WITHDRAWN

D1266373

B161089

AAY-4900
VC Grad

LIFE CYCLES

Activities for
Helping Children Live with
Daily Change and Loss

By Jeanne Lagorio

WITHDRAWN

Empowerment in Action
Carlsbad, CA 92009

LIFE CYCLES Grades K–6
Activities for Helping Children
Live with Daily Change and Loss

© Empowerment in Action 1991, 1997
© Zephyr Press 1993
Empowerment in Action, revised printing 1997
Printed in the United States of America

ISBN 0-9633195-0-7

Photographs by Mark and Dean Tucker,
Awakening Heart Productions,
used with permission

Editors: Stacey Lynn and Stacey Shropshire
Cover Design: Michelle Gallardo
Book Design: Nancy Taylor

Empowerment in Action
P.O. Box 3064
Carlsbad, CA 92009

All rights reserved. No form of this work may
be reproduced, transmitted, or recorded without
written permission from the publisher.

Library of Congress Cataloging-in-Publication Data

Lagorio, Jeanne, 1963–
     Life cycles: activities for helping children to live with
     daily change and loss / by Jeanne Lagorio.
          p.   cm.
     Includes bibliographical references.
     ISBN 0-9633195-0-7
     1. Loss (Psychology) in children. 2. Grief in children.
     3. School psychology. I. Title
     BF723.L68L34   1993
     155.9'3–dc20   92-33575

This book printed on recycled paper.

Acknowledgments

Teresa: Thanks for helping to make this possible. Your tenacity, ability to type quickly, and pleasant disposition have been wonderful.

Karl: Thanks for your love, suggestions, and ability to transform work into play, but most of all, for having faith in me.

Mom and Dad: Thanks for everything you've done over the years. Together you have complemented my life in wonderful ways.

Mary: Thanks for believing in me and my writing and for typing me through college free of charge. What a precious gift!

I also thank my forefathers and mothers for providing us with the freedom of speech, and I thank God for all the blessings in my life and work.

Dedication

This manual is dedicated to the children I have worked with who have experienced major losses. You have all imprinted my life in a very special way. It is my hope that this manual will assist and empower future children who will inevitably experience similar losses.

Contents

INTRODUCTION

Why I Developed This Program

During my graduate studies at the Jane Addams School of Social Work, University of Illinois, I had the opportunity to spend many days working with children who were misbehaving or were learning impaired. Seventy-five percent of my case load comprised children who were dealing with recent loss or had not completed the grieving process.

It is no longer rare for children to suffer significant losses. Cancer is the third leading cause of death in the United States, and as of April 1991, AIDS had killed over 10,000 Americans. Now children worry about their own mortality at a much earlier age than they used to. In addition, the rising divorce rate means that more children are experiencing loss now than in previous generations. Children from divorced homes lose their intact nuclear families, and in some cases see very little or nothing of one parent.

These observations helped me recognize the urgent need to help adults educate children about loss. I began developing this program out of a desire to serve my clients and others who were struggling with the same issues.

A great deal has been written on the psychological effects of loss and separation that can occur during childhood. Freud himself attributed much psychiatric illness to unexpressed pathological mourning. He was the first to focus on the importance of childhood experiences (Goldhaber 1986). John Bowlby, a specialist in childhood grief, notes that grief is complicated for children because the fear of separation from their parents is so intense. A loss may disrupt children's stable routine, and the grieving of those around them may be overwhelming. For these reasons, children may feel that a loss threatens their own survival. Research has led Bowlby to conclude that unsuccessfully mourned childhood losses create many common clinical disorders, varying in severity from fear of intimacy and impaired parenting ability to anxieties, phobias, depression, and suicide (Goldhaber 1986). Margaret Mahler's psychoanalytic literature on child development places a great deal of importance on the process of separation-individuation as a basis of ego development. Separation-individuation is a process that continues throughout childhood and, in a modified manner, into adulthood. When separation is not successfully accomplished for any reason, including the loss of the person from whom one is separating, ego development is impaired. Such disturbances as psychosis, character disorders, anxiety disorders, and obsessive disorders result (Goldhaber 1986).

The Purpose of the Program

As children learn how to cope with small daily losses effectively, they will build the necessary skills to help them cope with more significant losses. They can learn to view death as a final stage of growth rather than a regression or limitation. This program presents a gentle way to help children understand that loss and death are a natural part of life. It is designed to accommodate the needs of teachers and other helping professionals. The simple step-by-step format allows teachers to implement the program in the classroom, and other helping professionals will also appreciate this format. Though the units are geared toward children, they are not limited to this age group. I have modified the units for my work with adults and had great success.

To ensure that parents understand the objective of the unit, I suggest that the person using the program send a letter home explaining the program and its purpose. A copy of the list of children's grieving signs (pages 4–5) would be a useful accompaniment. This gesture educates parents, creates rapport between the parents and the teacher or counselor, and allows parents the opportunity to participate. Parents can then communicate any behavioral changes they note in their children to the teacher or counselor.

As you work through the program, you may find that feelings surface in the children that you were not expecting. You must understand that you did not create the feelings but instead helped them to surface; no feelings will arise that were not there, possibly unnoticed, to begin with. When you help children to identify the problem that is causing the feeling, they can address and resolve it. Unidentified problems only prolong pain and create other difficulties.

It is only natural that you might fear death or feel uncomfortable discussing it. Death is the unknown, and resistance to and fear of death are common. Also common is trying to keep yourself or others from going through a grieving process by saying such things as "Be strong," "Those things happen to everybody," or "You just have to forget about it and go on," or by doing such things as prematurely replacing a pet that has died. This program teaches more appropriate, helpful responses to someone who has suffered a loss.

General Program Information

Since children's cognitive and emotional development varies greatly according to chronological age, the program is divided into three groups: K–1, 2–4, and 5–6. Before the activities given for each group is a brief description of children that age, their level of development, and their perception of death.

The program is designed so the individual sessions in the 2–4 and 5–6 sections can last anywhere from fifty minutes to one and a half hours. The seven sessions may be split into weekly classes or run for seven consecutive days. I know it is difficult to find time to include programs other than general studies, but shortening every class by five minutes will make implementing this program possible.

The basic format remains the same in most sessions, and there is a selection of activities in each. As you begin to explore more significant losses, this manual will provide specific activities for you to use as a focus. These activities will allow the children to explore and express their feelings privately in a classroom but more intensely in a therapeutic setting.

Understanding Children and Grief

Children show signs of grieving differently from adults. They do not grieve steadily. They also may appear to be unaffected by loss, perhaps going out to play after hearing that someone significant to them has died. They may become defensive and appear brazen and uncaring, perhaps even joking about the loss. Rather than crying, a child may manifest his or her grief in one of the following ways:

- Cognitive—preoccupation, disorganized thinking, decline in academic performance, worrying about surviving family members, confusion

- Physical—complaining of illness (often of symptoms or ailments the deceased experienced), loss of appetite, sleeplessness or other sleep disorders, headaches

- Behavioral—acting out, withdrawing, truancy, overeating or undereating, daydreaming

- Emotional—guilt, fear of intimacy, anger, sadness, loneliness

Children are likely to act out or withdraw in response to loss because *they do not have the vocabulary necessary to express their grief verbally.* They need adults to help them develop a vocabulary for their experiences. Adults can identify and label feelings for children. Adults who are the most effective in helping children grieve are those who model clear communication and acceptance of emotional expression.

Children's Understanding of Death

3–6 years: Children this age have a poor concept of time and permanence; to them, death is not permanent.

6–9 years: Children this age realize that death exists and is final, but they believe that it happens only to other people and others' loved ones.

9 and up: Children understand that death is irreversible and are able to understand their own mortality; they may fear death.

How Teachers Can Help

- *Be aware* of the symptoms listed above and communicate closely with the family and school social worker/counselor.

- *Be available* so the child can have someone to talk with about the death. Most important, acknowledge the child's feelings, even the confused feelings. Just as you would want your beliefs and feelings to be honored, provide the same courtesy to children.

- *Check with the family* so you understand what happened and you can deal with any misconceptions the child may have.

- *Writing assignments down on paper* for the bereaved child is a small task that can help the child stay organized in this time of confusion and reorganization. Whenever a family member dies, all family members experience a role adjustment and readjustment.

- *Touch* the child appropriately from time to time to relieve tension. Put your hand on his or her shoulder, touch his or her arm or head. Give the child plenty of time to play and release physical tension.

- If a child is having difficulty with organization, *ask a "student buddy"* to assist the child with school work. A "teacher buddy" can provide emotional support if the child needs it.

- *Be aware of your personal feelings* regarding loss and death so you can be objective. Don't worry if you fear death or are uncomfortable discussing it. Identify and discuss your beliefs and feelings with someone you trust.

- *Be aware that grieving is a process.* It is normal to have recurring feelings of pain after a significant loss, especially during the first year. Although the pain will lessen with time, it is apt to recur throughout one's life. Pain is especially likely to occur during significant and milestone moments in one's life.

KINDERGARTEN AND FIRST-GRADE PROGRAM

Background

According to respected Swiss psychologist Jean Piaget, children 2 1/2 to 6 years of age have common characteristics of thought (Goldhaber 1986). Their view of the world is based primarily on outward appearances of events. For example, it is very difficult to explain to young children that two halves of a cookie are the same cookie; children see the halves as two differ- ent cookies. As a result of their limited cognition, they often see the cause of death erroneously, basing it on fictional circum- stances or the appearance of the moment. Children this age have not yet developed the ability to view situations objectively. They believe that inanimate objects have the same motives, feelings, and interactions as they do, and they believe the dead continue to eat, sleep, and play, as they do. It is also possible for children this age to believe that something they thought or did caused the death.

Children in this age group are also active, with short attention spans. They learn through movement and exploration. According to Erikson, a prominent psychologist, their activities serve mainly to develop initiative and to avoid feelings of guilt (Goldhaber 1986). It is especially important for adults who interact with children of this age to distinguish between behavior and the children themselves when correcting them so that children don't doubt their competency or feel guilty about who they are.

Because of the limited cognitive abilities and attention span of children within this age group, a classroom format is not appropriate. It is of greater value to allow children the freedom to express themselves and to work through their feelings with movement and play. After they experience a loss, children may also regress to skills they had previously mastered in order to feel a sense of security. Providing play time to review these skills will empower the children and reassure them that adult support is there for them.

Opening

Because of the limited cognitive ability and vocabulary of children in this age group, the following activities should be used as they are needed rather than in a structured, progressive format. Their purpose is to help these children experience different emotions, because learning at this age takes place on an emotional level.

Before beginning an activity, develop group agreements or review established agreements. Explain that the activity will involve group participation, so it is important that people respect one another, cooperate, and be responsible for themselves. Ask the children what guidelines would be helpful. Do not list more than five. Too many guidelines can be ineffective and confusing. Write them in simple language.

At the beginning of each class or session, display the list of guidelines in a place where everyone can see it. It will serve as a reminder. Some people find it helpful to review the agreements before each activity. Do what is natural for you.

SAMPLE AGREEMENT LIST

- Be responsible for yourself.
- Respect one another.
- Cooperate; do what is best for the group.

Suggested Activities

ACTIVITY 1: Hide-and-Seek Variation

Objective

To help children build trust in others by providing a situation that demonstrates consistency and predictability

Materials

None

This variation of hide-and-seek differs from the traditional game in that it is not competitive. The tone is not "try to catch me," but rather "help find me," and it is therefore supportive for the child.

- Select one child to be the hider. If there are any possible hiding places in the room that are not safe, be sure you tell the hider that those places are off limits.

- Have the class or group wait in the hall while the hider finds a place to hide.

- Tell the other children that they are going to pretend that the person hiding is lost and must be found as quickly as possible to ensure his or her safety. In a worried tone, express concern for the child who is hiding. Encourage the other children to do the same. Have fun with it! The children will quickly rush to the hider's rescue.

- Repeat the process until each student has had a chance to hide and experience being rescued.

ACTIVITY 2: Magic Tunnel

Objective

To help children express secret desires and help them understand that wishing and hoping can be a positive way of coping with a situation, but that the wishes and hopes do not necessarily change the outcome of a situation

Materials

6 or more chairs that children can crawl underneath
Crayons
2 or 3 sheets and/or blankets
Hand-held mirror or full-length mirror
Box to hold hand-held mirror

- Arrange chairs in a straight or curved line. The longer the tunnel, the better; it feels like more of a journey.

- Cover the chairs with sheets or blankets if possible to add to the illusion of a tunnel.

- Make up a story that reflects the purpose of the activity. The following is a story you might use to help participants get in touch with something they are wishing for:

The magic tunnel you are about to crawl through leads you to a land where wishes are heard. When you come out of the tunnel into this land, whisper your wish into the ear of the person who is there to greet you. [You will be waiting at the exit of the tunnel to hear the children's wishes.] *Now begin thinking of your wish and, one by one, crawl through the magic tunnel.*

To keep the children who have completed their journey occupied, have them draw pictures of how life will be when their wishes come true.

You may want to expand the activity by having a discussion about wishes. Tell the children that sometimes wishes don't come true. For example, there are times when a loved one, either a person or a pet, is hurt so badly or is so ill that he or she dies. Explain that no matter how hard the children wish, they cannot change the hurt or illness or the outcome.

- For the next story, without letting the participants see what you are doing, set up the full-length mirror and cover it with a sheet, blanket, cloth, or paper that serves as a veil, or place the hand-held mirror in a box and cover the box.

This story helps students build self-worth:

> *The magic tunnel you will crawl through is going to lead you to a land where a special person lives.*

As children exit the tunnel, you will be there to ask them if they would like to meet a very special person. If they say yes, have them say the magic words, "I would like to meet a very special person." Grant the child permission to raise the veil or open the box after he or she says the magic words.

To keep the children who have completed their journey through the tunnel occupied, have them draw themselves doing something they are good at or like about themselves. This activity will continue to build the children's self-worth.

- Conclude the activity by requesting feedback from the children.

ACTIVITY 3: Class Story

Objective
For children to express their anxieties and fantasies in an environment that helps them realize these feelings are normal

Materials
Butcher paper
Markers

- Have the entire class or group participate in writing a story. Fasten butcher paper to a wall, and as the children tell their story, transcribe it onto the butcher paper. Give the story a title, and if time permits, act it out.

  The following is a list of suggested story topics:
    - A family loses its dog.
    - A child their age loses his/her favorite toy.
    - A brother or sister of a child their age gets married and leaves home.

- A child their age has a parent who goes to war.

- A child their age has a pet that dies.

- A family has started recycling; why?

- A family separates due to divorce.

- Guide the story by asking the children questions about the people involved. Focus on feelings and what happens next, and work toward developing full characters and a full story line.

ACTIVITY 4: Good-bye–Welcome Back

Objective
To help children build trust in others by providing a situation that demonstrates consistency and predictability

Materials
1 large sheet or blanket

After a significant loss occurs or when a family is under stress due to trauma such as divorce, chronic illness, or war, the child needs to be reassured that someone will be there to keep his or her world intact. For others not experiencing a significant loss, this activity is a fun and reassuring experience.

- Take a large sheet and have each child hold on along the edge.

- Introduce the game by explaining that the group are going to play a good-bye–welcome back game. One child will be in the center under the sheet.

- Have the children lift the sheet and say good-bye to the child in the center, then lower the sheet and quickly raise it, welcoming the child in the center back.

- Conclude by explaining that sometimes people don't come back, such as when they die, but other people will be there for the child.

ACTIVITY 5: Peek-a-Boo

Objective
To reassure children and help them build trust

Materials
None

After a significant loss occurs or when a family is under stress due to such things as divorce, chronic illness, or war, the child needs to be reassured that someone will be there to keep his or her world intact.

- Take a few minutes to initiate a playful game of peek-a-boo with a struggling child. You can do so spontaneously with no materials.

ACTIVITY 6: Reading

Objective
To gain an understanding of coping with loss through storytelling

Materials
Books from list in Appendix B or other appropriate books

- Review books that deal with the concept of death or loss, and pay close attention to how the concept is portrayed. A list of suggested books follows, but you may want to review them first or use some that are not on my list.

REVIEWING SUGGESTIONS

- Your comfort level is important. Review the book to determine whether or not it is within your comfort level. You need to be able to discuss, easily and confidently, different feelings the characters in the story experience.

- *Be sure the books show both positive and negative emotions being accepted.* The books I suggest have been reviewed and meet this criterion.

- Think about how the book may affect certain students based on whether or not they have experienced losses similar to those presented in the book. If you have reservations, talk with the school social worker, psychologist, counselor, or someone else you trust.

- Read and discuss the stories with your class.

SUGGESTED STORIES

(a brief synopsis of each book is included in Appendix B)

Nonna by J. Bartoli (10 minutes)

First Snow by Helen Coutant (15 minutes)

Nana Upstairs and Nana Downstairs by T. DePaola
(18 minutes)

My Grandpa Died Today by J. Fassler (5 minutes)

When Violet Died by M. Kantrowitz (5 minutes)

Lifetimes by Bryan Mellonie and Robert Ingpen (7 minutes)

My Grandson Lew by C. Zolotow (5 minutes)

Saying Goodbye by Jim Boulden (coloring book)

NOTE: It is important to mention during the discussion that as we grow older, we may remember people or pets that have died and feel pain again. This is a normal part of the grieving process.

You may also want to use your creativity and experience to create games for your class or group that meet their special needs.

ACTIVITY 7: I'm Growing Up

Objective
To help children acknowledge their personal accomplishments and experience themselves as part of the life cycle

Materials
One or a few baby pictures of each student

This exercise illustrates to children their involvement in the life cycles of change. Children feel empowered when they are able to identify things that they can now accomplish easily that they could not accomplish earlier in their lives. The activity also reinforces the natural progression of skills that accompany maturation.

- Ask the children to bring one or a few baby pictures of themselves to the group.

- Have each child, one at a time, show the pictures to the group, talk about them, and complete the following statement:

I remember when I couldn't _____ and now I can.

SECOND-, THIRD-, AND FOURTH- GRADE PROGRAM

Background

According to Piaget, children 7 to 10 years of age are aware of transitions (Goldhaber 1986). Being aware of transitions enables them to see a relationship between two states. They understand the concept of reversibility. For example, these children are able to distinguish that the amount of water in a short glass is the same amount when poured into a tall glass, even though it looks like less in the tall glass. Children also understand that planted seeds mature into plants. This level of thought allows children a more sophisticated understanding of their world than was previously possible.

Eric Erikson notes that the main task of children 7 to 11 years of age is to develop a sense of industry and to avoid a sense of inferiority. Their industriousness is an indication of their awareness that they are now in the larger world and of their desire to be accepted by that world (Goldhaber 1986). Children are proud of their accomplishments and often value themselves through what they can produce. If children this age fail to feel this sense of industry due to the inability to stop a death or other loss, they develop instead a sense of inferiority or inadequacy.

Nine-year-old children are able to grasp the finality of death. However, they usually associate death with old people, other people, and with the disintegration of the body. According to Betty Staley, author of *Between Form and Freedom*, though, children 8 to 10 can experience a separation of the soul (Goldhaber 1986). In other words, they come to sense that they are their own selves with independent thoughts and feeling. The realization that their adored parents aren't perfect is confusing and upsetting. This confusion can lead to feelings of loss and concern about their parents' death.

Children of this age are naturally very interested in the details of burials and funerals. You need to answer their questions honestly and simply. I encourage you to allow children to choose whether or not to attend these events, because children interpret not being included as punishment. By allowing them to attend if they wish, you acknowledge and empower them. Attending also helps to curb their wild imaginations.

Since children of this age have a greater ability to deal with events in context, the curriculum material can explore more deeply. Their growing sense of competency and feelings of equality further support this exploration.

Opening

Explain the purpose of the group by saying, "We are going to meet on seven occasions to learn about life, death, and life cycles." Before going further, develop group agreements or review established agreements. Explain that many of the activities in these sessions will involve group participation, so it is important that people respect one another, cooperate, and be responsible for themselves. Ask the children what guidelines would be helpful. Do not list more than five. Too many guidelines can be ineffective and confusing. Write them in simple language.

At the beginning of each group session, display the list of guidelines in a place where everyone can see it. It will serve as a reminder. Some people find it helpful to review the agreement before each unit. Do what is natural for you.

SAMPLE AGREEMENT LIST

- Be responsible for yourself.

- Respect one another.

- Cooperate; do what is best for the group.

Session 1

Topic
Change as a natural part of our day and a natural part of the life cycle

Objective
To have the children become aware of the many changes and losses they cope with daily and to empower them through awareness and knowledge

Materials
Butcher paper
Chalk
1 marker

Discussion

- To begin, ask if anyone knows what a life cycle is. Listen to responses and explore the phrase "life cycle" further by explaining that it can be defined as two separate words.

- On the chalkboard, write *life,* and at a distance but on the same level, write *cycle*. Ask the group to define the terms *life* and *cycle*. Some examples follow:

LIFE	**CYCLE**
Opposite of death	Round
Growth	Movement
Breathing	Goes and comes back

- Develop the discussion further by asking the following questions and adding children's responses to the list. Feel free to use your experience and your understanding of and relationship with the children to elicit input from the group.

How do you know when something is alive?

What cycles have you seen change?

Some examples of answers follow:

LIFE	**CYCLE**
Things that are alive change. *people*—baby-child-adult-elderly caterpillar-cocoon-butterfly	**Seasons move in cycles.** winter-spring-summer-fall
Things that are alive heal. scratched knee sad feelings go away	**Holidays move in cycles.** Hanukkah Ramadan Christmas-Easter- Thanksgiving
Things that are alive need love and attention. Plants need water and sunlight. Animals need food and to be petted.	**Age moves in cycles.** Every year we get older and we come back to another birthday.
Things that are alive breathe. plants animals people	**Weather moves in cycles.** rain sun snow seasons
Things that are alive grow. *bird eggs*—birds *seeds*—plants	**Recycling moves in cycles.** Metal is taken from the Earth and made into a can or something else, then is recycled into another metal object.

Things that are alive need food.
people—three balanced meals
animals—plants, other animals,
    water
plants—water, air, sunshine

A wheel moves in cycles.
If you tape a spoke on
    your bike wheel, you
    will see this.

- Point out to the children that the "life" and "cycle" lists on the board are of changes that are continuous. We let go of them and they come back.

- Now on the board generate a new list of things that change and don't come back or don't come back the same after each cycle. Some examples are given below:

SOME THINGS CHANGE AND
DON'T COME BACK THE SAME

We let go of our baby teeth to allow room for permanent adult teeth to grow.

We grow out of smaller clothes to fit into bigger clothes.

We let go of one age to rise to another.

People's eyesight can change. They may need eyeglasses or contacts to see accurately.

When a pet dies, it is never to return except in memory.

When a person dies, he or she is never to return except in memory.

When people lose their hair, it usually does not grow back (exception: cancer patients undergoing chemotherapy).

Suggested Activities

ACTIVITY 1: The "Me" Cycle

Objective

For the children to understand the life cycle by seeing themselves as a part of the cycle

Materials

Paper
Crayons

Time Needed

Approximately 5 to 10 minutes

- Ask the children to draw themselves as babies, draw themselves now, and draw themselves as adults.

- When they complete this activity, ask for volunteers to share their pictures.

ACTIVITY 2: Cycles in Action

Objective

For children to use their imaginations and bodies to experience part of the life cycle, gaining a greater understanding of life's processes and changes

Materials

None

Time Needed

Approximately 5 to 10 minutes

- Divide the children into groups of 2 to 4.
- Assign each group a "cycle of change" to act out. A list of suggestions follows:
    - A human life
    - The life of a bird
    - The process of a caterpillar changing into a butterfly

- Seasons

- Day and night

● Give the children 10 to 15 minutes to prepare.

The children do not all have to be actors; some can be in charge of sound effects or production.

Session 2

Topic
The process one goes through when experiencing loss

Objective
To enable children to understand the stages of grief modified from the stages identified by Elisabeth Kübler Ross and to empower the children by helping them understand that their feelings are normal

Opening

Review what you covered in session 1. Ask the children if they have any questions or comments; discuss questions or comments before beginning session 2.

Introduce the topic by explaining that the group will be talking about what happens when we lose something: what we do first and how we feel, what we do second and how we feel, etc.

Discussion

● Ask if anyone has experienced a loss today or in the past few days. Some examples might be

- Lunch money

- Wanting something but not getting it

- Losing at a video game

- Getting a "C" rather than an "A" on a test

- If no one has experienced a loss in the past few days, ask the children what losses they remember from earlier in their lives. Some examples are

    - Losing a tooth

    - Losing Mom or Dad in a store

- Choose a loss that almost all the children have experienced so that they can visualize the situation.

- Once you have chosen a situation, ask the child who volunteered the information to recall what he or she did first, how he or she felt after doing it, what he or she did second, how he or she felt then, and so on. Continue until the child explains how the situation was resolved.

According to Elisabeth Kübler Ross, an authority on the grief process, individuals progress through five stages of grief after a loss:

1. Denial

2. Anger

3. Bargaining

4. Depression

5. Acceptance

People's emotional development and their relationship with those they lose determine the intensity and duration of each stage. I have substituted the following stages to make them more accessible to children and to help teachers use them in the classroom:

1. Confusion

2. Sadness, anger, and fear

3. Search for a solution

4. Acceptance

- Explain to the children that all people have similar feelings after experiencing a loss and that we all go through the same stages. Start the discussion by giving an example, such as a child who gets a "D" on a test for which she or he has studied:

    1. The child is *confused* about how this could have happened. Did the teacher make a mistake?

    2. The child begins to feel *sad, angry,* or maybe *frightened* about how her or his parents will react.

    3. The child begins to think about ways to *change the situation*. The child may see if the teacher graded the test correctly, ask to do extra credit, or ask to retake the test.

    4. After exploring possible solutions and realizing that the situation cannot be changed, the child eventually *accepts* the grade and releases the feelings about it.

- After you have given the example, use the following guidelines for a group discussion about the four stages of loss.

CONFUSION (DENIAL)	SADNESS, ANGER, AND FEAR (ANGER AND DEPRESSION)
Where did it go? Where did I put that? Retrace steps	These feelings are interchangeable depending on the individual.

SOLUTION SEARCH (BARGAINING)	ACCEPTANCE (ACCEPTANCE)

I will take care of it
  next time.
It's not my fault!
Whom can I talk to?
	I let go.
	I continue with daily life.
	From the experience, I
	  learned what I can do
	  differently next time.

- Invite the children to participate using their own experiences and examples.

- Highlight the similarities and differences in the children's responses.

- Accept all reactions to loss. If a child shares a response that is potentially unsafe, discuss other options of dealing with the loss. If the child's response concerns you, discuss it with a helping professional.

- Explain that change causes loss and the pain that results is called grief. Explain that sometimes we grieve for a long time because some things are very important to us, and we can't let go or forget about them easily. Eventually, we have to accept that our time with a loved one is over and that the time we shared was a gift. Clarify that acceptance means acknowledging that a situation cannot be changed or reversed, but that it does not mean we stop feeling pain. It is normal to have recurring feelings of pain. We cannot always define our emotions easily; they can be bittersweet.

- To help children feel empowered, note the many losses we experience and accept every day. For example, at night we say good-bye to the activities of the day and say hello to night. We must accept that it is time to go to sleep, even if we don't want to. There are times when we have to let go of people and things just as we let go of night and day.

- Discuss examples of daily letting go that the children share.

Choose one of the following activities.

ACTIVITY 1: Cartoon

Objective
For children to understand the stages they go through when they experience a loss and to help them become aware of the choices they have

Materials

8 1/2"- x -11" paper
Crayons
Markers

Time Needed

Approximately 10 to 15 minutes

- Take the piece of paper and fold it in half and in half again, then open it so you have one piece of paper with four rectangles, each rectangle representing one of the stages of grief.

- Ask the children to remember something they have lost or to imagine losing something. Then have them draw actual or made-up pictures of themselves going through the four stages of grief.

- It is important for the children to control what they draw in the last box. The resolution is empowering and it allows children to acknowledge their fantasies.

ACTIVITY 2: Collage of Change

Objective

For children to explore their feelings about different situations that involve change

Materials

Butcher paper or other large paper (If you have time, cut the paper in the shape of a circle. This shape reinforces the concept of change being part of a cycle.)

- Have the children cut pictures and words that depict change out of magazines and newspapers and bring the pictures to the group. Have the children paste the pictures on the paper.

- Next to the pictures, have the children write words or draw faces that depict their feelings.

NOTE: You can do the collage as a group on one large sheet of paper or individually on smaller sheets of paper. If you choose to do the group project, use the opportunity to discuss the children's pictures with them. If you choose to do an individual project, ask for volunteers to share their projects with the group at the end of the activity.

ACTIVITY 3: The "What Do I Do When I Lose Something" Book

Objective
To help children understand the stages they experience during loss and help them understand their reactions to loss

Materials
8 1/2"- x -11" or larger paper
Markers or crayons

Time Needed
Approximately 30 minutes

- Make books with four or more pages.

- Ask the children to remember something they have lost or to imagine losing something. Then have them draw actual or made-up pictures of themselves going through the four stages of grief.

- It is important for the children to control what they draw in the last box. The resolution is empowering and it allows children to acknowledge their fantasies.

Session 3

Topic
The many different feelings one has when experiencing the death of a loved one or other loss

Objective

To empower children to accept their own feelings as
well as the feelings of others by answering their questions
about loss

Opening

Review what you covered in session 2. Ask the children if they
have any questions or comments; discuss questions or comments
before beginning session 3.

Introduce the topic by explaining that change causes loss and
the pain that results is called grief. Explain that sometimes we
grieve for a long time because some things are very important to
us, and we can't let go of them easily. Explain also that what is
easy for one person to let go of may be difficult for another to let
go of. Sometimes losing someone or something hurts so much
that we try not to think about it, but not thinking about the loss
does not make the pain go away; not thinking about the loss only
hides the pain. Eventually, we have to accept that our time with a
loved one is over and that the time we shared was a gift. Clarify
that acceptance means acknowledging that a situation cannot be
changed or reversed, but that it does not mean we stop feeling
pain. It is normal to have recurring feelings of pain. Our feelings
can be bittersweet.

The difficulty in accepting a loss comes from our need to gain
control in a situation where we are powerless. Ask the children to
give an example of a loss and how someone might feel about it. If
they do not come up with an example, use the following scenario:

> *Moving to a new home and away from our friends, school,
> and neighborhood is a loss because we leave all that is
> familiar to us. We may feel sad, mad, or afraid about
> moving, but eventually we have to accept that we must go
> to the new place. At times we may think of what we left
> behind and feel pain. This pain is normal. It is part of the
> natural grieving process and may recur for a number of
> years or even a lifetime, although the duration and intensity
> will subside.*

One way to help children explore the feelings associated with the loss of a loved one is to read them a story about someone who is experiencing a loss. A story gives a child enough distance to experience loss in a nonthreatening way. Having someone read a story is also a soothing and nurturing experience for people of all ages.

ACTIVITY 1: Reading

Objective
To help children understand how people cope with loss through storytelling

Materials
A book from the list below

Time Needed
Approximately 10 to 40 minutes

- Read one of the stories listed below aloud to the group.

- Identify and discuss the different feelings the characters in the story experience and discuss how the author depicts loss as part of the life cycle. Discussion questions are in Appendix A.

BOOK LIST

- *The Fall of Freddie the Leaf* by Leo Buscaglia (10 minutes; this book is also available on audio tape)

- *Annie and the Old One* by Miska Miles (15 minutes)

- *The Tenth Good Thing about Barney* by Judith Viorst (5 minutes)

- *Growing Time* by Sandol Stoddard Warburg (40 minutes)

If time permits, read E. B. White's *Charlotte's Web* to the group. The time needed will vary depending upon the reader's ability and the group's attention span. This wonderful story is also available on video cassette.

REVIEWING SUGGESTIONS

- Review the book to determine whether or not you are comfortable with it. You need to be able to discuss, with ease and confidence, different feelings the characters in the story experience.

- Pay close attention to how the author presents the concept of death and loss. Be sure the characters accept both positive and negative emotions. The books I suggest have been reviewed and meet this criterion.

- Think about how the book may affect certain children based on whether or not they have experienced losses similar to those presented in the book. If you have reservations, talk with the school social worker, psychologist, counselor, or someone else you trust.

- Read the stories to your group and discuss them.

ACTIVITY 2: "The Black-and-White Forest"

Objective
To help children gain an understanding of coping with loss through guided imagery

Materials
"The Black-and-White Forest" by Jeanne Lagorio, below

"The Black-and-White Forest" by Jeanne Lagorio is a guided imagery about a girl who lets go of her innocence to explore her inner and outer worlds, losing some things and gaining others through her experience. The story is rich in description, and children will paint the images in their minds.

This activity stimulates the right hemisphere of the brain. According to research, the right and left hemispheres of the brain serve radically different functions. The left hemisphere governs linear (analytical) thought; the right hemisphere governs spatial (integrative) thought. The majority of classroom instruction requires children to use the left hemisphere. A curriculum that combines right- and left-brain functions, however, gives children a more balanced and enjoyable education. This visualization activity offers children the opportunity to use their right brains. Notice which children do well and enjoy the exercise. Do the same children achieve poorly on written or reading work? If so, they may do better if you include more right-brain activities in your curriculum.

- Explain to the children that you will read a short story to them and that they are to keep their eyes closed (or open if they prefer).

- They are to listen carefully and imagine clear pictures of what is happening in the story. The children may find this request odd. Children seldom find it necessary to use their imaginations. In fact, television and computers do almost all of the imagining and directing for them.

- Tell the children that years ago, before TV was invented, children their age would circle around the radio, listen to stories, and paint pictures in their minds based on what they heard. Tell them that they are going to do the same thing while you read the story.

- Ask them to notice colors, smells, and tastes.

- The story can be read while children are seated at their desks or on the floor.

- After you finish the story, discuss the questions on pages 35–36, or have each child write down the answers to the questions.

The Black-and-White Forest

by Jeanne Lagorio

Once upon a time, there was a little girl who lived in a forest. This was a very different forest, different from all other forests, for it had no color. All the trees and all the animals and all the plants were black and white. The only thing in the forest that wasn't black or white was the little girl's beautiful long hair, which glistened auburn in the sunlight.

This little girl was friends with all the animals, plants, and trees of the forest. And though she loved them all, she secretly admired the deer and the lion. They were the two closest to her heart.

The little girl admired the deer because it was graceful. When the little girl looked into the deer's eyes, she was captured by the sensitivity that the deer's soul reflected.

The little girl admired the lion for his strength and courage. When she looked into the lion's eyes, she was captured by the sensitivity his soul reflected. Yet she was often surprised to see fear in the lion's eyes when he roared ferociously with anger. She never told him this because she respected his anger and did not want to hurt his pride. In the evening, she would cuddle up in his mane feeling protected and loved.

One day, when the little girl was playing, she stumbled upon the edge of the forest and saw something very strange. She saw square objects everywhere. And they all glistened with a multitude of colors.

This confused her for she knew of only one color, and that was the auburn of her hair. She stood there in awe and confusion for a long while. Then she ran excitedly back to her forest friends and asked them if they knew of the multicolored square objects. They all replied, "No."

When she asked the lion, he told her in a gruff voice, "Forget about it and come to rest in my mane as you always do, for you know you will be comfortable there." She dutifully did so.

In the morning, she found her friend the deer. The little girl
told the deer of her adventure to the edge of the forest. She asked
the deer if it knew of the multicolored objects. The deer replied
sweetly that no such place existed, for it had run every inch of
the forest and had never found such a place.

The little girl felt very sad, for she knew she had not imagined this place, and yet no one would acknowledge the possibility that it existed. So the little girl decided to investigate further
on her own. She spent the morning gathering fruits and nuts for
her journey. By noon, she was on her way.

Just as she reached the edge of the forest, she noticed a little
girl just like herself, playing. She walked up to her and asked
her what her name was. The new little girl smiled and replied,
"Lynn." They had a wonderful time playing together all afternoon, and Lynn answered all the little girl's questions regarding
this strange place. As night fell, Lynn had to leave for dinner.
Both girls felt sad and exchanged "thank-yous" for the wonderful stories they had shared.

The little girl was too tired to walk back through the forest,
so she spent the night where she and Lynn had played. She
dreamed of all the beauty she had seen and of her friends in the
forest. When she awoke, she felt sad, for she wanted to enlighten
her friends and make sure her home was just as beautiful. So she
decided to go to the paint store Lynn had told her about. She
traded her fruits and nuts for gallons and gallons of colored
paint and paintbrushes.

With this done, she ran home filled with joy. She went to her
favorite place and began to paint, giving the animals, trees, and
flowers the gift of color, which they had never experienced
before. Soon her friends appeared and told her how they had
missed her and were glad she was home.

She found some of her friends' reactions to the color rather
odd. They were afraid of the beautiful color. She assured them
that there was nothing to fear and continued to paint. Some of
them took longer than others to come out of hiding and adjust
to the change. Some of them are still hiding. The little girl knew
that to be true to herself, she must continue to paint. The others
would have to adjust with time. If they couldn't, they would
have to find a way to cope.

After many, many hours of painting, her dear lion friend appeared. He told her how proud he was of her for having the courage to go beyond the edge of the forest. The little girl was surprised that she now had the same quality she had admired in the lion. Together they rejoiced.

Soon after this, her dear friend the deer appeared. It told the little girl that it had been watching her paint and that her brush strokes were very graceful. The little girl was surprised that she now possessed a quality that she had admired in her deer friend. Together they rejoiced in their colorful home.

Upon retiring for the night, the little girl reflected on all she had learned in such a short time, and she was gently rocked to sleep by the contented pounding of her happy heart.

The little girl continues to paint and continues to grow.

"THE BLACK-AND-WHITE FOREST" QUESTIONS

1. What was it like to listen to a story with your eyes closed? How did you feel? What did you notice? Did you see colors, smell odors, or taste anything?

2. When the girl looked into the deer's eyes, what did she see? When she looked into the lion's eyes, what did she see? What qualities have you seen when looking into someone else's eyes? Whose eyes were they?

3. What where the glistening, multicolored objects? How did the girl feel when she discovered them?

4. How did the little girl's friends react to the news that she had seen multicolored objects at the edge of the forest? What stage of loss were they in? (Circle one of the following.)

    • shock/confusion

    • anger/sadness/fear

    • bargaining

    • acceptance

5. How do you think the little girl's friends felt when
    she was nowhere to be found? What stages of loss
    were they in?

    ● shock/confusion

    ● anger/sadness/fear

    ● bargaining

    ● acceptance

6. What did the little girl have to let go of before
    she could experience the wonder of a world with
    color? How do you think she felt?

7. In what different ways did the little girl's friends
    react to their changed forest? Be sure to include the
    lion's, the deer's, and the other animals' reactions.
    What stages of loss were they in? (circle one)

    ● shock/confusion

    ● anger/sadness/fear

    ● bargaining

    ● acceptance

Session 4

Topic
The many different feelings one has when experiencing the death of a loved one or other loss

Objective
To empower children to express their emotions in a safe environment

Opening

Review what you covered in session 3. Ask the children if they have any questions or comments; discuss questions or comments before beginning session 4.

Introduce the new topic by saying, "Today we are going to talk about things we have lost and how we felt about losing them."

- Ask if anyone has experienced a loss recently.

- Write the examples on the board.

- When you have a list of three or four examples, ask the children who volunteered the information if they can remember in what parts of their bodies they felt loss. At least some of the children may remember where in their bodies they felt loss, but if no one does, don't panic. Simply say that it is an unusual question and therefore requires thought. Explain to the group that you will give them time to think of the answer to the question in the next activity. If the children who volunteered the information are able to tell you where they felt loss, tell the group that they are all going to get the chance to find the special places in their bodies where they feel loss. Begin activity 1.

ACTIVITY 1: Thinking on Your Feet

Objective
For children to become aware of the connection between their minds and their bodies

Materials
None

Time Needed
Approximately 10 to 15 minutes

- Ask the children to stand and close their eyes.

- Once their eyes are closed, ask the children to think of a time when they lost something and to raise their hands when they have thought of it.

- Ask them to find the place in their bodies where they feel the loss, raising their hands when they have found it.

- Ask for volunteers to share their discoveries.

- Repeat the activity a few times, asking the children to think of a different loss each time.

- Close by having the children take their seats.

ACTIVITY 2: Thinking in Silence

Objective
For children to become aware of the connection between their minds and their bodies

Materials
Paper
Crayons, markers, or colored pencils

Time Needed
Approximately 10 to 15 minutes

- When they are seated, ask the children to close their eyes again and think of a time when they lost something or when something died and to raise their hands when they have thought of it.

- Have them open their eyes and then draw pictures of themselves on sheets of paper. They may draw stick figures, but cookie cutter–like figures would allow them more room to color.

- Have them choose colors that represent their feelings and color the drawings in the places where they felt the feelings.

- Also have them draw faces that depict either how they felt when they experienced the loss or how they feel now when they remember the loss.

Closing

- Discuss with the children the kinds of feelings the activity aroused and the different places they colored. I notice a lot of people feel fear in their knees, but some feel it in other areas of their bodies. Emphasize that there is no wrong part of the body in which to feel emotions.

- Explain to the children that sometimes when we are not feeling well, it is because we are holding a feeling inside. For example, children who are picked on may feel embarrassed or rejected and say they have a "yucky" or weak feeling in their stomachs. They may actually have a stomachache.

- Tell the children, "Something we can do to help ourselves feel better at those times is to talk silently to the part of our body that hurts. We can let it know we want it to feel better soon as well as reassure it that it will soon feel good again. The pain is not permanent but is part of the natural ebb and flow of life."

- Close the session by doing the "What's It All About?" activity.

CLOSING ACTIVITY: What's It All About?

Objective
To give children the opportunity to synthesize and integrate the material covered in this session

Materials

Paper
Crayons, markers, or colored pencils
(3 or more colors per child)

- Ask the children to complete the following
  statements on a piece of paper:

  I have learned   _____,

  I liked or disliked _____,

  and I observed   _____.

- Teaching children to use "I" statements helps
  empower them and helps them to synthesize
  material. Leave 5 minutes for children who are
  willing to share their statements.

Session 5

Topic

Learning strategies to cope with loss

Objective

To empower children to select safe ways of dealing with loss

Opening

Review what you covered in session 4. Ask the children if they
have any questions or comments; discuss questions and comments before beginning session 5.

Introduce the new topic by saying something such as, "Today
we are going to talk about safe ways of coping with stress." Start
by telling the children that they will be participating in a fun
exercise called "Drawing Feelings."

ACTIVITY 1: Drawing Feelings

Objective

For children to become aware of the ways in which they have
coped with fear, sadness, and anger in the past

- Have the children draw pictures that depict fear. Tell them to title the pictures "I feel afraid when . . . "

- After they finish their pictures, ask them what it was like to draw the pictures.

- Allow children to share their pictures if they wish.

- Do not attempt to probe for deeper feelings or discuss personal matters with the children. If you feel a child would benefit by seeing a social worker, counselor, or psychologist, please make the appropriate referral privately.

- After you have discussed fear fully, have the children repeat the activity using sadness, then anger, then worry. When the children have completed all four drawings and you have discussed each fully, ask the children to choose a picture they would like to change their feelings about and draw a new picture that reflects a new feeling.

- When they have finished these drawings, ask the children to share their experiences. Their comments will lead the group into the next activity.

ACTIVITY 2: Coping Strategies

Objective
To help children learn about the many choices they have to cope with loss

Materials
None

Time Needed
Approximately 5 to 10 minutes

- With your group, brainstorm a list of coping strategies on the chalkboard. Write "drawing" down first, or some other artistic activity that people use when they are upset. See how many different coping strategies the children can generate. Some examples follow.

COPING OPTIONS

- Drawing.

- Talking with a person, with a pet, or with a stuffed animal.

- Writing a letter that you do not intend to mail.

- Making a memory album.

- Making a commitment to amend a situation.

- Making a gratitude list.

- Keeping a daily or event journal of "moments worth expressing." Children may title their own journals.

- Putting together a feeling scrapbook. This scrapbook is based on the same concept as the journal except that children will add memorabilia from various places: newspapers, magazines, personal belongings, drawings, mementos, or pictures.

Closing

Time needed
Approximately 5 minutes

- Read "Sioux Indian Story" by Jamie Sams, below.

My grandfather took me to the fish pond on the farm when I was about seven, and told me to throw a stone into the water. He told me to watch the circles created by the stone. Then he asked me to think of myself as that Stone Person. "You may create lots of splashes in your life but the waves that come from those splashes will disturb the peace of all your fellow creatures," he said. "Remember that you are responsible for what you put in your circle and that your circle will also touch many other circles. You will need to live in a way that allows the good that comes from your circle to send the peace of that goodness to others. The splash that comes from anger or jealousy will send those feelings to other circles. You are responsible for both."

That was the first time I realized each person creates the inner peace or discord that flows out into the world. We cannot create world peace if we are riddled with inner conflict, hatred, doubt, or anger. We radiate the feelings and thoughts that we hold inside, whether we speak them or not. Whatever is splashing around inside of us is spilling out into the world, creating beauty or discord with all other circles of life.

- Point out that this is a good story about individuals who take responsibility for themselves and use safe, effective coping skills when they are troubled.

Session 6

Topic
Learning to cope with loss

Objective
To empower children to choose safe ways to deal with loss

Opening

Review what you covered in session 5. Ask the children if they have any questions or comments; discuss questions or comments before beginning session 6.

Tell the children that this is the second-to-the-last session. Introduce the topic by saying something such as, "Today we are going to brainstorm and experience safe ways of handling loss." Ask if anyone knows what brainstorming means and have a volunteer explain it to the group. Clarify that brainstorming means hearing ideas from everyone, which gives us the opportunity to learn about many different approaches and solutions to problems.

- With your group, generate a list on the board of ineffective and effective coping behaviors. Some examples are listed below.

Ineffective	*Effective*
Blaming others	Talking with someone
Blaming self	Asking for a replacement
Pretending the loss doesn't bother you	Writing a letter
	Making a memory album
Damaging something	Making a list of 5 to 10 good things about the lost person or object
Hitting someone	
Not talking	
Hiding	Making a feeling scrapbook
	Making an audio tape
	Allowing yourself to feel emotions when they arise

SUGGESTIONS TO ENHANCE
THE BRAINSTORMING PROCESS

- A child is waiting in line for a ride at a carnival and loses the turn because the ride needs repair. What might the child do to cope effectively and ineffectively in this situation?

- A pet is very ill and the veterinarian informs the family that the pet should be put to sleep. What might a child do to cope effectively and ineffectively in this situation?

When the children demonstrate that they are aware of the difference between ineffective and effective coping skills, have them role play effective behaviors in a series of vignettes.

ACTIVITY 1: Role Play

Objective
For children to feel the difference between using effective and ineffective coping strategies

Materials
None

Time Needed
Approximately 10 to 15 minutes to allow children to plan their skits and 40 minutes for the skits

- Divide children into groups of 4 or 5 and assign them a situation that requires them to respond to a loss.

- Designate one child with leadership qualities to monitor each group.

- Have the groups plan a skit that demonstrates ineffective responses first.

SCENE 1

Juan, who is ___ years old, blows out the tire on his bike. How might he react that would make the situation worse? What reactions would make the situation better?

SCENE 2

Mom tells Sally that the family pet has died. Sally is feeling very sad and lonely. What are some things that Sally can do that would not make her feel better or would make her feel worse? What can Sally do to make herself feel better?

SCENE 3

Reggie's older brother has gone to an out-of-state college and will be coming home only on holidays. Reggie misses his brother and the fun they had together. He liked playing ball with his brother after school. What might Reggie do that would make this situation worse? What might he do to improve the situation?

SCENE 4

Maria has a new baby brother that is 2 months old. Mom doesn't have time to play with Maria as she did before the baby was born. Maria is feeling angry and sad because she wants her family to be the way it used to be. What can she do that would make the situation worse? What can she do to make it better?

- Allow 5 to 7 minutes for each group to act out their skit.

Closing

Time Needed
Approximately 1 to 5 minutes

- Ask the children to write down one new positive strategy they learned to use in a situation that involves loss. Also have them write down how they feel physically when they use an effective coping strategy and how they feel when they use an ineffective strategy. Remind them that the unit will end next week.

ACTIVITY 2: Me and My Attitude

Objective
For children to experience that changing an attitude and perception can alter the outcome of a situation and lead to more problem-solving options

Materials
None

Time Needed
Approximately 40 minutes

- Have the children write down situations they are currently having difficulty with. The situations may include fighting with a sibling or not wanting to study for a test.

- Then have the children write down what they feel, what they think, and how they behave during their situations.

- Invite the children to develop a positive way of coping with their situations. Direct the children to close their eyes and imagine themselves interacting lovingly and positively with the people (including themselves) in their situations. For example, they may see themselves being considerate of people they frequently argue with, or they may see themselves feeling good while studying for a test.

- Allow the children 1 to 3 minutes to imagine themselves solving their problems effectively.

- After children have finished imagining the effective behavior, have them write about their experience answering some of the following questions:

  - How did your attitude affect the situation?

  - What effect did imagining your new attitude have on your body ?

  - What can you do to resolve your problem in the way you imagined?

- Explain that attitude can strongly influence the outcome of some situations. Following are two examples of shifts in attitude:

I don't want to give up my TV show, but it's not worth upsetting myself and possibly my family over. I will see if I can work out a compromise. Maybe we can tape one show while we are watching the other. Or perhaps I can keep busy with other things, such as a craft, homework, helping around the house, etc.

I usually do not like to study, but I do like getting good grades. Maybe studying will be different this time if I make a game of it or break up the study periods into 10- to 15-minute daily segments for one week.

Session 7

Topic
What children have learned from past losses and
how they can use this knowledge in future situations

Objective
To empower children to use their personal and
community resources

Opening

Review what you covered in session 6. Ask the children if they
have any questions or comments; discuss questions or comments
before beginning session 7.

Tell the children that today is the last session of the unit.
Introduce the new topic by saying something such as, "We have
spent a lot of time discussing the many different feelings people
have when they experience loss and how those feelings can
influence behavior. Today we are going to talk about what we
have learned from our own experiences of loss and how we can
apply that knowledge in future situations."

Discussion

- Draw the following diagram on the chalkboard.
  Explain the roles each group plays in the
  children's lives and that the roles are interrelated.
  Emphasize that children can go to any group for
  help. For example, if a child leaves a lunch on the
  bus, she or he may go to the school office and ask
  the secretary for help. The two of them may
  decide to call someone at the child's home and ask
  that person to bring a new lunch to school. If no
  one is able to bring a lunch, the child may ask
  friends to share their lunches. Point out that many
  people may try to solve a problem before someone
  finds a solution.

- Move on to the next activity.

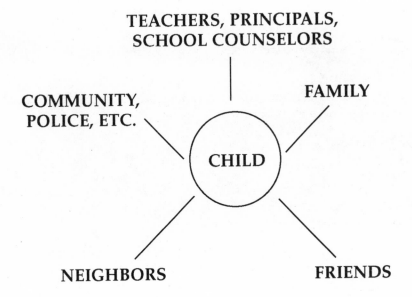

ACTIVITY 1: Important Helpers

Objective
To teach the children about many of the resources available in times of need

- Make enough copies of the "Important Helpers List" (page 51) for each child to have one. (Two are included; copy the page and cut in half.) Have the children fill out their lists. The lists will have names and phone numbers of people the children can call for help.

- Encourage the children to add to the list. Have phone books available for those children who do not know the numbers of people or agencies that the children want to add to their lists. You may want to allow the children to contact their parents during the activity period so they can complete the list.

- Tell the children you will place the lists in a safe
  and accessible place. Ask for their input when you
  discuss where the lists could be placed.

CLOSING: Evaluation

Objective
To have children synthesize and integrate the material covered
in the seven-week program

Materials
8 1/2"-x-11" paper
Pencils

Time Needed
Approximately 10 to 15 minutes

- Have the children write a story about or draw a
  picture of what they liked about the unit, what
  they disliked, and what their favorite memory
  of the unit is.

Important Helpers List

1. Mother–Home Phone # _____ Work # _____

2. Father–Home Phone # _____ Work # _____

3. Grandparents or other relatives

   Home Phone # _____ Work Phone # _____

4. Friends–Phone # _____ Phone # _____

5. Police–Phone # _____

6. Fire Department–Phone # _____

7. Children's Hot Line*–Phone # _____

8. School Social Worker/Psychologist*–Phone # _____

- -

Important Helpers List

1. Mother–Home Phone # _____ Work # _____

2. Father–Home Phone # _____ Work # _____

3. Grandparents or other relatives

   Home Phone # _____ Work Phone # _____

4. Friends–Phone # _____ Phone # _____

5. Police–Phone # _____

6. Fire Department–Phone # _____

7. Children's Hot Line*–Phone # _____

8. School Social Worker/Psychologist*–Phone # _____

* These numbers should be particularly accessible. The school counselor should have them on file.

FIFTH- AND SIXTH-GRADE PROGRAM

Background

According to Piaget, children begin to develop abstract thought and hypothetical and deductive reasoning around the age of eleven (Goldhaber 1986). They are able to develop a hypothesis, to consider solutions to problems based on the hypothesis, and to test the deductions systematically to determine if the hypothesis is valid. These complex thinking abilities continue to develop and to be refined throughout adulthood. These abilities, however, are not enough for children to solve real-life problems successfully. Children also become increasingly aware of their sexuality and of death and individual mortality.

Erikson notes that twelve-year-old children are beginning to develop a sense of identity that continues to develop throughout adolescence (Goldhaber 1986). Maturing cognitive abilities and the emergence of introspective qualities are hallmarks of this stage of development. As a result, children become much more effective at processing information. These self-reflective skills make the emergence of a true self-concept possible.

Children in this stage also seek greater autonomy; in essence, they seek to be trusted. They long for parents and peers to respect their decision-making abilities. Children also know the teacher's authority stops at the playground. The belief that "being grown up" means obeying adults begins changing as children explore their self-identity. For example, children of this age begin to keep secrets as a means to exercise their autonomy. According to Betty Staley, children this age are also learning to become comfortable with the depths of their inner, private worlds and with their outer, public transactions (Goldhaber 1986). Children this age often learn by feeling.

Opening

Explain the purpose of the group by saying, "We are going to meet on seven occasions to learn about life, death, and life cycles." Before going further, develop group agreements or review established agreements. Explain that many of the activities in these sessions will involve group participation, so it is important that people respect one another, cooperate, and be responsible for themselves. Ask the children what guidelines would be helpful. Do not list more than five. Too many guidelines can be ineffective and confusing. Write them in simple language.

At the beginning of each session, display the list of guidelines in a place where everyone can see it. It will serve as a reminder. Some people find it helpful to review the agreement before each unit. Do what is natural for you.

SAMPLE AGREEMENT LIST

- Be responsible for yourself.

- Respect one another.

- Cooperate; do what is best for the group.

Session 1

Topic
Change as a natural part of our day and a natural part
of the life cycle

Objective
To have the children become aware of the many changes
and losses they cope with daily and to empower them through
awareness and knowledge

Materials
Butcher paper
Chalk
1 marker

Discussion

- To begin, ask if anyone knows what a life cycle is.
  Listen to responses and explore the phrase "life
  cycle" further by explaining that it is a phrase that
  can be defined as two separate words.

- On the chalkboard, write *life,* and at a distance but
  on the same level, write *cycle.* Ask the group to
  define the terms *life* and *cycle.* Some examples
  follow:

LIFE	CYCLE
Opposite of death	Round
Growth	Movement
Breathing	Goes and comes back

- Develop the discussion further by asking the
  following questions and adding children's
  responses to the list. Feel free to use your
  experience and your understanding of and
  relationship with the children to elicit input
  from the group.

How do you know when something is alive?

What cycles have you seen change?

Some possible answers follow:

LIFE	CYCLE
Things that are alive change.	**Seasons move in cycles.**
people—baby-child-adult-elderly	winter-spring-summer-fall
caterpillar-cocoon-butterfly	
Things that are alive heal.	**Holidays move in cycles.**
scratched knee	Hanukkah
sad feelings go away	Ramadan
	Christmas-Easter-
	Thanksgiving
Things that are alive	**Age moves in cycles.**
need love and attention.	Every year we get older
Plants need water and sunlight.	and we come back to
Animals need food and to	another birthday.
be petted.	
Things that are alive breathe.	**Weather moves in cycles.**
plants	rain
animals	sun
people	snow
	seasons
Things that are alive grow.	**Recycling moves in cycles.**
bird eggs—birds	Metal is taken from the
seeds—plants	Earth and made into a
	can or something else,
	then is recycled into
	another metal object.
Things that are alive need food.	**A wheel moves in cycles.**
people—three balanced meals	If you tape a spoke on
animals—plants, other animals,	your bike wheel, you
water	will see this.
plants—water, air, sunshine	

- Point out to the children that the "life" and "cycle" lists on the board are of changes that are continuous. We let go of them and they come back.

- Now on the board generate a new list of things that change and don't come back or don't come back the same after each cycle. Some examples are given below:

SOME THINGS CHANGE AND
DON'T COME BACK THE SAME

We let go of our baby teeth to allow room for permanent adult teeth to grow.

We grow out of smaller clothes to fit into bigger clothes.

We let go of one age to rise to another.

People's eyesight can change. They may need eyeglasses or contacts to see accurately.

When a pet dies, it is never to return except in memory.

When a person dies, he or she is never to return except in memory.

When people lose their hair, it usually does not grow back (exception: cancer patients undergoing chemotherapy).

Suggested Activities

ACTIVITY 1: The "Me" Cycle

Objective
For the children to understand the life cycle by seeing themselves as a part of the cycle

Materials
Paper
Crayons

Time needed
Approximately 5 to 10 minutes

- Ask the children to draw themselves as babies, draw themselves now, and draw themselves as adults.

- When they complete this activity, ask for volunteers to share their pictures.

ACTIVITY 2: Those Who Have Made a Difference

Objective
To help children understand the impact other individuals have had on the children's lives and development and the interconnectedness of all things

- Ask the children to make a list of the significant people in their lives, past and present. Their lists might include the person who taught them how to ride a bike, blow a bubble, or the one who really allows them to laugh and let go.

- Have them choose one person that they feel influenced them the most and have them give their reasons for choosing that person.

- Also have the children write whether the special person is still in their lives or not.

- Once they have come up with reasons for their choices, ask for volunteers to comment on their lists, discussing specifically how each list reflects life-cycle changes. For example, did the chosen person move? Did he or she grow distant because personal interests changed? If the person taught the child a skill, did it lead to more freedom, more responsibility, or both? Will the memory endure a lifetime of changes?

Session 2

Topic
The process one goes through when experiencing loss

Objective
To enable children to understand the stages of grief modified from the stages identified by Elisabeth Kübler Ross and to empower the children by helping them understand that their feelings are normal

Opening

Review what you covered in session 1. Ask the children if they have any questions or comments; discuss questions or comments before beginning session 2.

Introduce the topic by explaining that the group will be talking about what happens when we lose something: what we do first and how we feel, what we do second and how we feel, etc.

Discussion

- Ask if anyone has experienced a loss today or in the past few days. Some examples might be

  - Lunch money

  - Getting lost on the way to a friend's house

  - Wanting something but not getting it

  - Losing at video games

  - Getting a "C" rather than an "A" on a test

- If no one has experienced a loss in the past few days, ask the children what losses they remember from earlier in their lives. Some examples are

  - Losing a tooth

  - Losing Mom or Dad in a store

- Choose a loss that almost all the children have
  experienced so that they can visualize the
  situation.

- Once you have chosen a situation, ask the child
  who volunteered the information to recall what
  he or she did first, how he or she felt after doing it,
  what he or she did second, how he or she felt then,
  and so on. Continue until the child explains how
  the situation was resolved.

According to Elisabeth Kübler Ross, an authority on the grief
process, individuals progress through five stages of grief after a
loss:

1. Denial

2. Anger

3. Bargaining

4. Depression

5. Acceptance

People's emotional development and their relationship with
those they lose determine the intensity and duration of each
stage. I have substituted the following stages to make them
more accessible to children and to help teachers use them in
the classroom:

1. Confusion

2. Sadness, anger, and fear

3. Search for a solution

4. Acceptance

- Explain to the children that all people have similar
  feelings after experiencing a loss and that we all go
  through the same stages. Start the discussion by
  giving an example, such as a child who gets a "D"
  on a test for which she or he has studied:

1. The child is *confused* about how this could have happened. Did the teacher make a mistake?

2. The child begins to feel *sad, angry,* or maybe *frightened* about how her or his parents will react.

3. The child begins to think about ways to *change the situation.* The child may see if the teacher graded the test correctly, ask to do extra credit, or ask to retake the test.

4. After exploring possible solutions and realizing that the situation cannot be changed, the child eventually *accepts* the grade and releases the feelings about it.

● After you have given the example, use the following guidelines for a group discussion about the four stages of loss.

CONFUSION
(DENIAL)

Where did I go?
Where did I put that?
Retrace steps

SADNESS, ANGER,
AND FEAR
(ANGER AND DEPRESSION)

These feelings are inter-
changeable depending
on the individual.

SOLUTION SEARCH
(BARGAINING)

I will take care of it
next time.
It's not my fault!
Whom can I talk to?

ACCEPTANCE
(ACCEPTANCE)

I let go.
I continue with daily life.
From the experience, I
learned what I can do
differently next time.

● Invite the children to participate using their own experiences and examples.

● Highlight the similarities and differences in the children's responses.

- Accept all reactions to loss. If a child shares a response that is potentially unsafe, discuss other options of dealing with the loss. If the child's response concerns you, discuss it with a helping professional.

- Explain that change causes loss and the pain that results is called grief. Explain that sometimes we grieve for a long time because some things are very important to us, and we can't let go or forget about them easily. Eventually, we have to accept that our time with a loved one is over and that the time we shared was a gift. Clarify that acceptance means acknowledging that a situation cannot be changed or reversed, but that it does not mean we stop feeling pain. It is normal to have recurring feelings of pain. We cannot always define our emotions easily; they can be bittersweet.

- To help children feel empowered, note the many losses we experience and accept every day. For example, at night we say good-bye to the activities of the day and say hello to night. We must accept that it is time to go to sleep, even if we don't want to. There are times when we have to let go of people and things just as we let go of night and day.

- Discuss examples of daily letting go that the children share.

Choose one of the following activities.

ACTIVITY 1: Cartoon

Objective
For children to understand the stages they go through when they experience a loss and to help them become aware of the choices they have

Materials
8 1/2"-x-11" paper
Crayons
Markers

Time Needed
Approximately 10 to 15 minutes

- Take the piece of paper and fold it in half and in half again, then open it so you have one piece of paper with four rectangles, each rectangle representing one of the stages of grief.

- Ask the children to remember something they have lost or to imagine losing something. Then have them draw actual or made-up pictures of themselves going through the four stages of grief.

- It is important for the children to control what they draw in the last box. The resolution is empowering and it allows children to acknowledge their fantasies.

ACTIVITY 2: Collage of Change

Objective
For children to explore their feelings about different situations that involve change

Materials
Butcher paper or other large paper (If you have time, cut the paper in the shape of a circle. This shape reinforces the concept of change being part of a cycle.)

- Have the children cut pictures and words that depict change out of magazines and newspapers and bring the pictures to the group. Have the children paste the pictures on the paper.

- Next to the pictures, have the children write words or draw faces that depict their feelings.

  NOTE: You can do the collage as a group on one large sheet of paper or individually on smaller sheets of paper. If you choose to do the group project, use the opportunity to discuss the children's pictures with them. If you choose to

do an individual project, ask for volunteers to
share their projects with the group at the end of
the activity.

ACTIVITY 3: Collage of Personal Change

Objective
To help children explore their feelings about their personal
experiences involving loss and change

- Follow the directions for activity 2, "The Collage
  of Change," but have the children add personal
  belongings such as photographs, poems, fabric,
  and other trinkets to the paper.

ACTIVITY 4: The "What Do I Do When
I Lose Something?" Book

Objective
To help children understand the stages they experience during
loss and help them understand their reactions to loss

Materials
8 1/2"-x-11" or larger paper
Markers or crayons

Time Needed
Approximately 30 minutes

- Make books with four or more pages.

- Ask the children to remember something they
  have lost or to imagine losing something. Then
  have them draw actual or made-up pictures of
  themselves going through the four stages of grief.

- It is important for the children to control what
  they draw in the last box. The resolution is
  empowering and it allows children to
  acknowledge their fantasies.

ACTIVITY 5: Research Project

Objective

To help children learn how other cultures perceive and honor death, expanding the children's framework for dealing with death

- Tell the children that they will be doing a small research project together. Explain that they will explore how other cultures and religions deal with loss. People from different parts of the world and different religions have different views about what happens after death and how the dead should be honored.

- Allow the children to divide themselves into groups of 3 or 4.

- Write the selection of cultures on the board and ask if any group would like to study a particular culture. If so, assign it to the group. A group may be enthusiastic about a culture not listed on the board. Allow the children to discuss a topic they find interesting with you, and if it is appropriate, approve it.

SUGGESTED TOPICS

- Native American culture

- Japanese culture

- African tribal cultures

- Chinese culture

- Indian culture

- Eskimo culture

- Jewish customs and traditions

- Catholic customs and traditions

Allow the children to use the rest of the period to get started on the research project.

CLASS PRESENTATIONS

- Discuss the results of the children's research with
  them. Be sure to stay neutral and support all
  beliefs. Point out that although people's beliefs
  and ceremonies may differ, we all agree that life
  changes form. A fact that adults and children need
  to accept is that no one really knows what happens
  after death. What is important is that there are
  many possibilities, that we may choose to believe
  the one that feels right for us, and that it may
  change over time.

Session 3

Topic
The many different feelings one has when experiencing
the death of a loved one or other loss

Objective
To empower children to accept their own feelings as well as
the feelings of others by answering their questions about loss

Opening

Review what you covered in session 2. Ask the children if they
have any questions or comments; discuss questions or comments
before beginning session 3.

Introduce the topic by explaining that change causes loss and
the pain that results is called grief. Explain that sometimes we
grieve for a long time because some things are very important to
us, and we can't let go of them easily. Explain also that what is
easy for one person to let go of may be difficult for another to let
go of. Sometimes losing someone or something hurts so much
that we try not to think about it, but not thinking about the loss
does not make the pain go away; not thinking about the loss only
hides the pain. Eventually, we have to accept that our time with
a loved one is over and that the time we shared was a gift.
Clarify that acceptance means acknowledging that a situation

cannot be changed or reversed, but that it does not mean we stop feeling pain. It is normal to have recurring feelings of pain. Our feelings can be bittersweet.

The difficulty in accepting a loss comes from our need to gain control in a situation where we are powerless. Ask the children to give an example of a loss and how someone might feel about it. If they do not come up with an example, use the following scenario:

> *Moving to a new home and away from our friends, school, and neighborhood is a loss because we leave all that is familiar to us. We may feel sad, mad, or afraid about moving, but eventually we have to accept that we must go to the new place. At times we may think of what we left behind and feel pain. This pain is normal. It is part of the natural grieving process and may recur for a number of years or even a lifetime, although the duration and intensity will subside.*

One way to help children explore the feelings associated with the loss of a loved one is to read them a story about someone who is experiencing a loss. A story gives a child enough distance to experience loss in a nonthreatening way. Having someone read a story is also a soothing and nurturing experience for people of all ages.

ACTIVITY 1: Reading

Objective
To help children understand how people cope with loss through storytelling

Materials
A book from the list below

Time Needed
Approximately 10 to 40 minutes

- Read one of the stories listed below aloud to the group.

- Identify and discuss the different feelings the characters in the story experience and discuss how

the author depicts loss as part of the life cycle.
Discussion questions are in Appendix A.

GROUP BOOK LIST

- *Annie and the Old One* by Miska Miles (15 minutes)
- *The Tenth Good Thing about Barney* by Judith Viorst (5 minutes)
- *Growing Time* by Sandol Stoddard Warburg (40 minutes)
- *Sadako and the Thousand Paper Cranes* by Eleanor Coerr (40 minutes)
- *I, Monty* by Marcus Bach (50 minutes)

INDIVIDUAL BOOK LIST

- *Thank You, Jackie Robinson* by Barbara Cohen
- *Hang Tough, Paul Mather* by Alfred Slote
- *Three-Legged Race* by Charles Crawford (has some references to sexuality)

If time permits, read E. B. White's *Charlotte's Web* to the group. The time needed will vary depending upon the reader's ability and the group's attention span. This wonderful story is also available on video cassette.

REVIEWING SUGGESTIONS

- Review the book to determine whether or not you are comfortable with it. You need to be able to discuss, with ease and confidence, different feelings the characters in the story experience.

- Pay close attention to how the author presents the concept of death and loss. Be sure the characters accept both positive and negative emotions. The books I suggest have been reviewed and meet this criterion.

- Think about how the book may affect certain children based on whether or not they have experienced losses similar to those presented in the book. If you have reservations, talk with the school social worker, psychologist, counselor, or someone else you trust.

ACTIVITY 2: Group Book Presentations

Objective
To help children become more aware of other people's feelings and reactions to loss

- Get copies of all the books on the book list on page 68. Divide the children into groups of 3 or 4 and have each group choose one of the books from the book list.

- Have the group choose one of the following activities to explore different feelings the characters experience in the story. If possible, the children should also explore their own feelings.

  - book report

  - shoe box panorama

  - cartoon

  - skit

  - poster

  - rap

  - collage

  - video

  - activity created by the group

- If time permits, devote one period to group presentations. If time does not permit, have the children turn in their work one week after the assignment has been given.

ACTIVITY 3: "The Black-and-White Forest"

Objective
To help children gain an understanding of coping with loss
through guided imagery

Materials
"The Black-and-White Forest" by Jeanne Lagorio, below

"The Black-and-White Forest" by Jeanne Lagorio is a guided
imagery about a girl who lets go of her innocence to explore her
inner and outer worlds, losing some things and gaining others
through her experience. The story is rich in description, and
children will paint the images in their minds.

This activity stimulates the right hemisphere of the brain.
According to research, the right and left hemispheres of the brain
serve radically different functions. The left hemisphere governs
linear (analytical) thought; the right hemisphere governs spatial
(integrative) thought. The majority of classroom instruction
requires children to use the left hemisphere. A curriculum that
combines right- and left-brain functions, however, gives children
a more balanced and enjoyable education. This visualization
activity offers children the opportunity to use their right brain.
Notice which children do well and enjoy the exercise. Do the
same children achieve poorly on written or reading work? If so,
they may do better if you include more right-brain activities in
your curriculum.

- Explain to the children that you will read a short
  story to them and that they are to keep their eyes
  closed (or open if they prefer).

- They are to listen carefully and imagine clear
  pictures of what is happening in the story. The
  children may find this request odd. Children
  seldom find it necessary to use their imaginations.
  In fact, television and computers do almost all of
  the imagining and directing for them.

- Tell the children that years ago, before TV was
  invented, children their age would circle around
  the radio, listen to stories, and paint pictures in
  their minds based on what they heard. Tell them

that they are going to do the same thing while you
read the story.

- Ask them to notice colors, smells, and tastes.

- The story can be read while children are seated at
  their desks or on the floor.

- After you finish the story, discuss the questions on
  pages 73–74, or have each child write down the
  answers to the questions.

The Black-and-White Forest

by Jeanne Lagorio

Once upon a time, there was a little girl who lived in a forest.
This was a very different forest, different from all other forests,
for it had no color. All the trees and all the animals and all the
plants were black and white. The only thing in the forest that
wasn't black or white was the little girl's beautiful long hair,
which glistened auburn in the sunlight.

This little girl was friends with all the animals, plants, and
trees of the forest. And though she loved them all, she secretly
admired the deer and the lion. They were the two closest to her
heart.

The little girl admired the deer because it was graceful. When
the little girl looked into the deer's eyes, she was captured by the
sensitivity that the deer's soul reflected.

The little girl admired the lion for his strength and courage.
When she looked into the lion's eyes, she was captured by the
sensitivity his soul reflected. Yet she was often surprised to see
fear in the lion's eyes when he roared ferociously with anger. She
never told him this because she respected his anger and did not
want to hurt his pride. In the evening, she would cuddle up in his
mane feeling protected and loved.

One day, when the little girl was playing, she stumbled upon the edge of the forest and saw something very strange. She saw square objects everywhere. And they all glistened with a multitude of colors.

This confused her for she knew of only one color, and that was the auburn of her hair. She stood there in awe and confusion for a long while. Then she ran excitedly back to her forest friends and asked them if they knew of the multicolored square objects. They all replied, "No."

When she asked the lion, he told her in a gruff voice, "Forget about it and come to rest in my mane as you always do, for you know you will be comfortable there." She dutifully did so.

In the morning, she found her friend the deer. The little girl told the deer of her adventure to the edge of the forest. She asked the deer if it knew of the multicolored objects. The deer replied sweetly that no such place existed, for she had run every inch of the forest and had never found such a place.

The little girl felt very sad, for she knew she had not imagined this place, and yet no one would acknowledge the possibility that it existed. So the little girl decided to investigate further on her own. She spent the morning gathering fruits and nuts for her journey. By noon, she was on her way.

Just as she reached the edge of the forest, she noticed a little girl just like herself, playing. She walked up to her and asked her what her name was. The little girl smiled and replied, "Lynn." They had a wonderful time playing together all afternoon, and Lynn answered all the little girl's questions regarding this strange place. As night fell, Lynn had to leave for dinner. Both girls felt sad and exchanged "thank-yous" for the wonderful stories they had shared.

The little girl was too tired to walk back through the forest, so she spent the night where she and Lynn had played. She dreamed of all the beauty she had seen and of her friends in the forest. When she awoke, she felt sad, for she wanted to enlighten her friends and make sure her home was just as beautiful. So she decided to go to the paint store Lynn had told her about. She traded her fruits and nuts for gallons and gallons of colored paint and paintbrushes.

With this done, she ran home filled with joy. She went to her favorite place and began to paint, giving the animals, trees, and flowers the gift of color which they had never experienced before. Soon her friends appeared and told her how they had missed her and were glad she was home.

She found some of her friends' reactions to the color rather odd. They were afraid of the beautiful color. She assured them that there was nothing to fear and continued to paint. Some of them took longer than others to come out of hiding and adjust to the change. Some of them are still hiding. The little girl knew that to be true to herself, she must continue to paint. The others would have to adjust with time. If they couldn't, they would have to find a way to cope.

After many, many hours of painting, her dear lion friend appeared. He told her how proud he was of her for having the courage to go beyond the edge of the forest. The little girl was surprised that she now held the same quality she had admired in the lion. Together they rejoiced.

Soon after this, her dear friend the deer appeared. She told the little girl that she had been watching her paint and that her brush strokes were very graceful. The little girl was surprised that she now possessed a quality that she had admired in her deer friend. Together they rejoiced in their colorful home.

Upon retiring for the night, the little girl reflected on all she had learned in such a short time, and she was gently rocked to sleep by the contented pounding of her happy heart.

The little girl continues to paint and continues to grow.

"THE BLACK-AND-WHITE FOREST" QUESTIONS

1. What was it like to listen to a story with your eyes closed? How did you feel? What did you notice? Did you see colors, smell odors, or taste anything?

2. When the girl looked into the deer's eyes, what did she see? When she looked into the lion's eyes, what did she see? What qualities have you seen when looking into someone else's eyes? Whose eyes were they?

3. What where the glistening, multicolored objects?
    How did the girl feel when she discovered them?

4. How did the little girl's friends react to the news
    that she had seen multicolored objects at the edge
    of the forest? What stage of loss were they in?
    (Circle one of the following.)

    - shock/confusion

    - anger/sadness/fear

    - bargaining

    - acceptance

5. How do you think the little girl's friends felt when
    she was nowhere to be found? What stages of loss
    were they in?

    - shock/confusion

    - anger/sadness/fear

    - bargaining

    - acceptance

6. What did the little girl have to let go of before she
    could experience the wonder of a world with
    color? How do you think she felt?

7. In what different ways did the little girl's friends
    react to their changed forest? Be sure to include the
    lion's, the deer's, and the other animals' reactions.
    What stages of loss were they in? (circle one)

    - shock/confusion

    - anger/sadness/fear

    - bargaining

    - acceptance

Session 4

Topic
The many different feelings one has when experiencing the death of a loved one or other loss

Objective
To empower children to express their emotions in a safe environment

Opening

Review what you covered in session 3. Ask the children if they have any questions or comments; discuss questions or comments before beginning session 4.

Introduce the new topic by saying, "Today we are going to talk about things we have lost and how we felt about losing them."

- Ask if anyone has experienced a loss recently.

- Write the examples on the board.

- When you have a list of three or four examples, ask the children who volunteered the information if they can remember in what parts of their bodies they felt loss. At least some of the children may remember where in their bodies they felt the loss,

but if no one does, don't panic. Simply say that
it is an unusual question and therefore requires
thought. Explain to the group that you will give
them time to think of the answer to the question in
the next activity. If the children who volunteered
the information are able to tell you where they felt
loss, tell the group that they are all going to get the
chance to find the special places in their bodies
where they feel loss. Begin activity 1.

ACTIVITY 1: Thinking on Your Feet

Objective
For children to become aware of the connection between their
minds and their bodies

Materials
None

Time Needed
Approximately 10 to 15 minutes

- Ask the children to stand and close their eyes.

- Once their eyes are closed, ask the children to think
  of a time when they lost something and to raise
  their hands when they have thought of it.

- Ask them to find the place in their bodies where
  they feel the loss, raising their hands when they
  have found it.

- Ask for volunteers to share their discoveries.

- Repeat the activity a few times, asking the children
  to think of a different loss each time.

- Close by having the children take their seats.

ACTIVITY 2: Thinking in Silence

Objective
For children to become aware of the connection between their
minds and their bodies

Materials
Paper
Crayons, markers, or colored pencils

Time Needed
Approximately 10 to 15 minutes

- When they are seated, ask the children to close their eyes again and think of a time when they lost something or when something died and to raise their hands when they have thought of it.

- Have them open their eyes and then draw pictures of themselves on sheets of paper. They may draw stick figures, but cookie cutter–like figures would allow them more room to color.

- Have them choose colors that represent their feelings and color the drawings in the places where they felt the feelings.

- Also have them draw faces that depict either how they felt when they experienced the loss, or how they feel now when they remember the loss.

ACTIVITY 3: What's in the News

This activity helps children become aware that a larger world exists outside of the small world in which they live. The activity challenges them to empathize with others and makes them aware that news stories are about other people.

Objective
To help children gain an understanding of how world events can effect a sense of loss in individuals, communities, and nations

- Have the children locate and cut out a newspaper or magazine article about loss. Subjects may include a team losing a game, environmental concerns, natural disasters, or death.

- Have the children write short essays about the articles that answer the following questions:

- What is the loss?

- How does it affect the people involved, the community, and the world as a whole?

- Identify how the people in the story experience the stages of grief: confusion; sadness, anger, fear; search for a solution; and acceptance.

- How would you feel if you were in the situation?

- The article must be turned in with the written assignment.

Closing

- Discuss with the children the kinds of feelings activity 2 aroused and the different places they colored. I notice a lot of people feel fear in their knees, but some feel it in other areas of their bodies. Emphasize that there is no wrong part of the body in which to feel emotions.

- Explain to the children that sometimes when we are not feeling well, it is because we are holding a feeling inside. For example, children who are picked on may feel embarrassed or rejected and say they have a "yucky" or weak feeling in their stomachs. They may actually have a stomachache.

- Tell the children, "Something we can do to help ourselves feel better at those times is to talk silently to the part of our body that hurts. We can let it know we want it to feel better soon as well as reassure it that it will soon feel good again. The pain is not permanent, but is part of the natural ebb and flow of life."

- Close the session by doing the "What's It All About?" activity.

CLOSING ACTIVITY: What's It All About?

Objective
To give children the opportunity to synthesize and integrate the material covered in this session

Materials
Paper
Crayons, markers, or colored pencils
(3 or more colors per child)

- Ask the children to complete the following statements on a piece of paper:

  I have learned _____,

  I liked or disliked _____,

  and I observed _____.

- Teaching children to use "I" statements helps to empower them and helps them to synthesize material. Leave 5 minutes for children who are willing to share their statements.

Session 5

Topic
Learning strategies to cope with loss

Objective
To empower children to select safe ways of dealing with loss

Opening

Review what you covered in session 4. Ask the children if they have any questions or comments; discuss questions and comments before beginning session 5.

Introduce the new topic by saying something such as, "Today we are going to talk about safe ways of coping with stress." Start by telling the children that they will be participating in a fun exercise called "Drawing Feelings."

ACTIVITY 1: Drawing Feelings

Objective

For children to become aware of the ways in which they have coped with fear, sadness, and anger in the past

- Have the children draw pictures that depict fear. Tell them to title the pictures "I feel afraid when . . . "

- After they finish their pictures, ask them what it was like to draw the pictures.

- Allow children to share their pictures if they wish.

- Do not attempt to probe for deeper feelings or discuss personal matters with the children. If you feel a child would benefit by seeing a social worker, counselor, or psychologist, please make the appropriate referral privately.

- After you have discussed fear fully, have the children repeat the activity using sadness, then anger, then worry. When the children have completed all four drawings and you have discussed each fully, ask the children to choose a picture they would like to change their feelings about and draw a new picture that reflects a new feeling.

- When they have finished these drawings, ask the children to share their experiences. Their comments will lead the group into the next activity.

ACTIVITY 2: Coping Strategies

Objective

To help children learn about the many choices they have to cope with loss

Materials

None

Time Needed

Approximately 5 to 10 minutes

- With your group, brainstorm a list of coping strategies on the chalkboard. Write "drawing" down first, or some other artistic activity that people use when they are upset. See how many different coping strategies the children can generate. Some examples follow.

COPING OPTIONS

- Drawing

- Talking with a person, with a pet, or with a stuffed animal

- Writing a letter that you do not intend to mail

- Making a memory album

- Making a commitment to amend a situation

- Making a gratitude list

- Keeping a daily or event journal of "moments worth expressing." Children may title their own journals.

- Putting together a feeling scrapbook. This scrapbook is based on the same concept as the journal except that children will add memorabilia from various places: newspapers, magazines, personal belongings, drawings, mementos, or pictures.

ACTIVITY 3: I Wish I Had . . .

Objective
To help children express and let go of secrets and unfulfilled wishes

Materials
Paper
Pencils or pens

Time Needed
Approximately 30 to 40 minutes

This activity allows children to verbalize any regrets and wishes they may have after experiencing a loss and to lessen the intensity of their longing. If they have not experienced a significant loss, use the exercise to give children time to think about what they would do in another situation.

If people can learn to avoid judging situations as either good or bad, right or wrong, they can learn lessons from the situations and will be less likely to repeat the same errors. When observation turns to judgment, people have the potential to become self-punishing. This exercise helps turn the "I should haves" into "I could haves."

- Have the children write a brief description of a situation in which they didn't do what they wanted to do. Then have them write down what they wish they had said or done.

- Collect the slips of paper and discuss ways to dispose of them as a group.

  - You may keep them in a special box.

  - The children can watch as you burn them.

  - You can recycle them.

  - You can make papier mâché out of them and the group can create a class sculpture.

- Choose one of the ways the group comes up with and dispose of the slips of paper.

- Talk with the children about allowing themselves to let their unfulfilled wishes dissolve and be transformed. Mention the importance of self-forgiveness and learning from experiences. Mention that if they cannot let go of their feelings and thoughts, they may want to confide in someone.

ACTIVITY 4: In Honor of . . .

Objective
To help children develop a means of acknowledging the deceased

This activity is a way to honor people or pets the children have lost. If they don't create some kind of memorial, children may hesitate to move forward for fear of forgetting about or not properly honoring the deceased.

- Ask the children to think of losses that deeply affected them.
- Once they identify the losses, ask the children to think of special ways in which they can honor the deceased. Some examples are
  - Planting a tree
  - Dedicating a wall in the school to the deceased person and painting it
  - Making a commitment to new behavior
  - Beading a necklace; each bead will represent a special wish, thought, or something the child is grateful for
  - Putting a special object that reminds the child of a lost person or pet in a special box, frame, etc.
  - Doing community service work
  - Developing a club at school that welcomes new children
- After the children have chosen ways to honor the deceased, have them turn in statements of action.

Closing

Time Needed
Approximately 5 minutes

- Read "Sioux Indian Story" by Jamie Sams, below.

My grandfather took me to the fish pond on the farm when I was about seven, and told me to throw a stone into the water. He told me to watch the circles created by the stone. Then he asked me to think of myself as that Stone Person. "You may create lots of splashes in your life but the waves that come from those splashes will disturb the peace of all your fellow creatures," he said. "Remember that you are responsible for what you put in your circle and that your circle will also touch many other circles. You will need to live in a way that allows the good that comes from your circle to send the peace of that goodness to others. The splash that comes from anger or jealousy will send those feelings to other circles. You are responsible for both."

That was the first time I realized each person creates the inner peace or discord that flows out into the world. We cannot create world peace if we are riddled with inner conflict, hatred, doubt, or anger. We radiate the feelings and thoughts that we hold inside, whether we speak them or not. Whatever is splashing around inside of us is spilling out into the world, creating beauty or discord with all other circles of life.

- Point out that this is a good story about individuals who take responsibility for themselves and use safe, effective coping skills when they are troubled.

Session 6

Topic
Learning to cope with loss

Objective
To empower children to choose safe ways to deal with loss

Opening

Review what you covered in session 5. Ask the children if they have any questions or comments; discuss questions or comments before beginning session 6.

Tell the children that this is the second-to-the-last session. Introduce the topic by saying something such as, "Today we are going to brainstorm and experience safe ways of handling loss." Ask if anyone knows what brainstorming means and have a volunteer explain it to the group. Clarify that brainstorming means hearing ideas from everyone, which gives us the opportunity to learn about many different approaches and solutions to problems.

- With your group, generate a list on the board of ineffective and effective coping behaviors. Some examples are listed below.

Ineffective	*Effective*
Blaming others	Talking with someone
Blaming self	Asking for a replacement
Pretending the loss doesn't bother you	Writing a letter
Damaging something	Making a memory album
Hitting someone	Making a list of 5 to 10 good things about the lost person or object
Not talking	Making a feeling scrapbook
Hiding	Allowing yourself to feel emotions when they arise

SUGGESTIONS TO ENHANCE
THE BRAINSTORMING PROCESS

- A child is waiting in line for a ride at a carnival and loses the turn because the ride needs repair. What might the child do to cope effectively and ineffectively in this situation?

- A pet is very ill and the veterinarian informs the family that the pet should be put to sleep. What might a child do to cope effectively and ineffectively in this situation?

When the children demonstrate that they know the difference between ineffective and effective coping skills, have them role play effective behaviors in a series of vignettes.

ACTIVITY 1: Role Play

Objective
For children to feel the difference between using effective and ineffective coping strategies

Materials
None

Time Needed
Approximately 10 to 15 minutes to allow children to plan their skits, and 40 minutes for the skits

- Divide children into groups of 4 or 5 and assign them a situation that requires them to respond to a loss.

- Designate one child with leadership qualities to monitor each group.

- Have the groups plan a skit that demonstrates ineffective responses first.

SCENE 1

Mario learns that his mother has cancer. He is shocked; he never knew she was ill. What ways could he react that might help the situation? What ways might make the situation worse?

SCENE 2

Mom tells Sally that the family pet has died. Sally is feeling very sad and lonely. What can Sally do to make herself feel better? What could she do that would not help her?

SCENE 3

Reggie's older brother has gone to an out-of-state college and will be coming home only on holidays. Reggie misses his brother and the fun they had together. He liked playing ball with his brother after school. What might Reggie do that would make this situation worse? What might he do to improve the situation?

SCENE 4

Maria has a new baby brother that is 2 months old. Mom doesn't have time to play with Maria as she did before the baby was born. Maria is feeling angry and sad because she wants her family to be the way it used to be. What can she do that would make the situation worse? What can she do to make it better?

SCENE 5

After a frustrating day at school, a boy or girl learns that a parent has been laid off. How could she or he react to help the situation? What reactions might make the situation worse?

- Allow 5 to 7 minutes for each group to act out their skit.

ACTIVITY 2: Pick a Solution

This activity exposes the children to many different coping options in a nonthreatening manner. It helps them realize their behavior is normal and makes them aware that some actions might be unsafe or harmful.

Objective
To help children realize they have many options and choices of ways to cope with loss

Materials
Paper
Pencils

- Have the children write down 1 to 3 ways they cope with loss. Make it clear that their names are not to be on the papers.

- Place all the papers in a container.

- One at a time, have each child draw a slip of paper from the container.

- Each child will hand the slip of paper to you and you will read it.

- Select one or more children to write the coping tactics on the board. Keep track of the number of times tactics are repeated by placing a mark under the behavior in the way illustrated:

I Kicked Something   **I Talked with Mom or Dad**

|| ||||

- Discuss the similarities and differences, potential danger and safety of each coping strategy. Continue to brainstorm other possibilities. If you need to, elicit participation with the following questions:

  - What do TV heroes do? (Some possible heroes may be Teenage Mutant Ninja Turtles, Doogie Howser, or Bart Simpson. You know your group and will know what examples they will relate to.)

- Is it realistic to use the coping techniques these characters use? Why or why not?

- If we had magic powers, how might those powers change our coping approach? What would we do?

ACTIVITY 3: The Musical Solution

Objective
To help children become aware of the connection between their bodies and minds and to illustrate coping techniques based on posture and movement

Materials
Celebrate Life audiocassette by Karl Anthony. (You can order this tape by calling 1-800-843-0165, or by writing to Anthony Music, P.O. Box 8878, La Jolla, CA 92038.)

Time Needed
Approximately 30 to 40 minutes

You can do this activity outside, in a large room, or in a classroom. If you are in a classroom, rearrange the desks so there is enough room for the children to move (approximately arm's distance or more between two children).

NOTE: As the facilitator, you can model ways that the body shows sadness, anger, and fear. Your getting involved enthusiastically in the activity can be more fun for you and the children.

- Ask the children to show sadness in their bodies. Most children will slouch, move slowly, and make weeping sounds. You may be pleasantly surprised at some of the children's original and creative expressions of sadness.

- After a few seconds, ask the children to exaggerate the sadness, and a few seconds later, ask them to exaggerate the sadness even more.

- Then have them listen to "Every Little Cell" on the tape and move their bodies in a happy way; remind them to respect each other's space and to be

responsible for themselves. After 30 seconds to 1
minute, stop the tape.

- Now instruct them to show anger in their bodies;
  make it clear that they are not to hurt themselves
  or anyone else, or to damage anything. Most
  children will scowl, make fists, and stamp their
  feet.

- Encourage them to act madder, and even madder
  still.

- Again, have the children listen to "Every Little
  Cell" and move their bodies in a happy way. After
  30 seconds to 1 minute, stop the tape.

- Now ask the children to show fear in their bodies.
  Most children will constrict, tremble, and cower.

- Encourage them to show more and more fear.

- Have them listen to "Every Little Cell" and show
  happiness in their bodies. Allow the good feelings
  and movements to continue until the song is over.

- When the song is over, have everyone sit down
  and discuss the activity. Use the following
  questions:

  - Did you like or dislike the activity? What did
    you like and dislike about it?

  - Did the music make you feel different? How?

  - When you feel sad or upset in some other
    way, does music make you feel different?
    How?

- Who makes music by tapping a pencil, hand, or
  foot when they are upset? Who sings?

It is important to point out that one way we can cope with
feelings is by moving our bodies, making music, or singing.
The next activity illustrates the power of coping with feelings
physically.

ACTIVITY 4: Feel Good, Feel Bad

Objective

To help children become aware of the connection between their minds and bodies and to illustrate coping techniques using posture and movement

Materials

None

- Ask the children to slouch and bow their heads.

- After a few seconds, instruct them to stand or sit up straight and lift their heads.

- Ask them if they feel different. How?

- Instruct them to repeat these movements rapidly as you repeat the commands "feel bad" and "feel good."

- After doing the exercise for approximately 30 seconds to 1 minute, ask if they feel different. How? Emphasize again how we can change our emotional state by moving physically.

- Ask the children when and in what situations moving can be an effective coping mechanism.

Session 7

Topic

What children have learned from past losses and how they can use this knowledge in future situations

Objective

To empower children to use their personal and community resources

Opening

Review what you covered in session 6. Ask the children if they have any questions or comments; discuss questions or comments before beginning session 7.

Tell the children that today is the last session of the unit. Introduce the new topic by saying something such as, "We have spent a lot of time discussing the many different feelings people have when they experience loss and how those feelings can influence behavior. Today we are going to talk about what we have learned from our own experiences of loss and how we can apply that knowledge in future situations."

Discussion

- Draw the following diagram on the chalkboard. Explain the roles each group plays in the children's lives and that the roles are interrelated. Emphasize that children can go to any group for help. For example, if a child leaves a lunch on the bus, she or he may go to the school office and ask the secretary for help. The two of them may decide to call someone at the child's home and ask that person to bring a new lunch to school. If no one is able to bring a lunch, the child may ask friends to share their lunches. Point out that many people may try to solve a problem before someone finds a solution.

- Move on to the next activity.

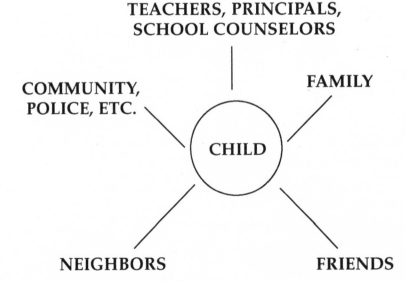

TEACHERS, PRINCIPALS, SCHOOL COUNSELORS

COMMUNITY, POLICE, ETC.

FAMILY

CHILD

NEIGHBORS

FRIENDS

ACTIVITY 1: Important Helpers

Objective

To teach the children about many of the resources available in times of need

- Make enough copies of the "Important Helpers List" (page 94) for each child to have one. (Two are included; copy the page and cut in half.) Have the children fill out their lists. The lists will have names and phone numbers of people the children can call for help.

- Encourage the children to add to the list. Have phone books available for those children who do not know the numbers of people or agencies that the children want to add to their lists. You may want to allow the children to contact their parents during the activity period so they can complete the list.

- Tell the children you will place the lists in a safe and accessible place. Ask for their input when you discuss where the lists could be placed.

CLOSING: Evaluation

Objective

To have children synthesize and integrate the material covered in the seven-week program

Materials

8 1/2"-x-11" paper
pencils

Time Needed

Approximately 10 to 15 minutes

- Have the children write a story about or draw a picture of what they liked about the unit, what they disliked, and what their favorite memory of the unit is.

Important Helpers List

1. Mother–Home Phone # _____ Work # _____

2. Father–Home Phone # _____ Work # _____

3. Grandparents or other relatives

    Home Phone # _____ Work Phone # _____

4. Friends–Phone # _____ Phone # _____

5. Police–Phone # _____

6. Fire Department–Phone # _____

7. Children's Hot Line*–Phone # _____

8. School Social Worker/Psychologist*–Phone # _____

9. Scout Leader–Phone # _____

10. Coach–Phone # _____

- -

Important Helpers List

1. Mother–Home Phone # _____ Work # _____

2. Father–Home Phone # _____ Work # _____

3. Grandparents or other relatives

    Home Phone # _____ Work Phone # _____

4. Friends–Phone # _____ Phone # _____

5. Police–Phone # _____

6. Fire Department–Phone # _____

7. Children's Hot Line*–Phone # _____

8. School Social Worker/Psychologist*–Phone # _____

9. Scout Leader–Phone # _____

10. Coach–Phone # _____

* These numbers should be particularly accessible. The school counselor should
have them on file.

APPENDIX A

Discussion Questions and Master Copies

When Violet Died

Discussion Questions

1. How did Eva find a way to make her cat live longer?

2. Is Eva really able to make the cat live longer or is she able to keep the memory alive longer?

3. Will each new cat be exactly the same as the one before because it has the same name?

4. What are some other ways we can keep memories of special people, animals, places, or things alive?

5. What do the children do for Violet after she dies to let her know she is important to them?

6. Do all the children feel the same at the funeral? How do they feel?

7. Is one person responsible for making all the arrangements, such as making the punch, getting a box, and writing the poem and song? How might the funeral be different if they don't work together?

8. Does anyone have anything to share?

Possible Answers

1. Eva decides to name all of her cat's kittens after their mother and to do this renaming forever.

2. Eva is able to make Violet live longer by keeping memories of her alive.

3. Reinforce the children's responses by using the example that one boy named Billy is different from another boy named Billy even though they have the same name. Each animal, plant, or person that is born is unique and special, just as each child is.

4. Examples: pictures, memorials, talking about the person, etc.

    We can keep memories in our hearts, too. We know the ones we are trying to remember are there because we can feel them. We also know we keep memories in our heads because we can remember what those we have lost looked like and things they have done. When our hearts and heads are working together, it's like being with those loved ones all over again.

5. Examples: Have a funeral, have a party, write and read a poem, write and sing a song, put her in a special box, find a special place to bury her.

6. It may be helpful to turn to pages 9–10 and 13–14.

    Examples: Eva is very sad.

    Billy is bored at times and wants to leave.

    Amy is in charge so it is more difficult to see her sadness.

    Do not limit the children's responses to what is mentioned above. They may perceive the situation differently and you need to validate their perceptions. Expand on their comments and reassure them that there is no right or wrong way to feel. Different people respond differently to loss.

7. Expand on the children's comments by emphasizing the importance of people working together, especially in times of loss. The funeral would not be the same if one person decided not to contribute. For example, it would be very different if Billy didn't bring the box or if Eva didn't sing her song. People working together makes experiences nicer or easier for everyone.

8. If children tell of their personal experiences, just listen and validate their feelings. Simply making eye contact, saying "uh-huh," and repeating what they have said are all ways to validate their feelings.

Nonna

Discussion Questions

1. How do the family members feel after they hear Nonna has died? What things happen to make us think they feel that way?

2. What are some of the things the family did with Nonna when she was alive that will change now that she has died?

3. In the story, no one says that this Christmas is the first the family has spent without Nonna. What do they do instead?

4. It is different not having Nonna there for Christmas, but the family has other special people with them to celebrate the holiday. Who are they?

5. After Nonna dies, the children each receive something of Nonna's as a gift. Who receives what and what other gift of Nonna's do they share?

6. What are some other ways we can remember special people or animals who have died?

Possible Answers

1. Examples: It gets quiet—shock; Mom burns dinner—preoccupied thoughts; everyone starts to cry—sad.

   Mention that people respond differently to loss and that there is no right or wrong way to respond.

2. Examples: The children went to Nonna's on Saturday to play and eat lunch, soup, and cookies; the uncles would go over for coffee and cookies as well as to see if there was anything they could do for Nonna; Nonna would sit in her favorite chair; Nonna and the children would sit and sing sometimes on the front porch swing.

   Point out to the class that they have just mentioned many ways in which Nonna has made a difference in the lives of her family members. These special moments will be kept in the memories of family members forever.

3. The youngest child bakes the cookies Nonna always baked. The other family members laugh with joy when they see the cookies.

4. In addition to the obvious, special guest (Tony), point out that each person at the table is really a special guest and would be missed if he or she were not there.

5. Examples: Tony receives Nonna's mandolin; Amy receives a quilt; the family shares produce from the garden with the neighbor; Amy learns to make Nonna's cookies.

6. Examples: Keep a picture of the loved one in view; take up a hobby the person enjoyed; talk to other people about the person.

Annie and the Old One

Discussion Questions

1. To what culture does Annie belong? What clues in the story lead you to your answer?

2. What activities do Annie and her grandmother do together that tell us they were important to one another?

3. What does Grandma mean when she says she will "go back to the earth" when the loom is finished?

4. What do the family members do after they hear the news that Grandma is going to die?

5. What things does Annie do to try and stop her Grandmother from dying?

6. Does Annie have the power to stop time? Why or why not?

Possible Answers

1. The family's traditions and customs are unique to Navajo culture.

2. Examples: Grandma tells Annie stories about when rains flooded the desert, when rains did not fall; they cook together; they laugh together when the mouse runs across the floor.

3. After you have waited for a response, clarify that it is the Navajo way of saying "Grandma will die soon." Further explain that "going back to the earth" means she will be buried in the earth. There she will help give nutrients to the earth and plants, which will in turn help other things grow.

4. Examples: Each family member receives a gift of something that belonged to Grandma, and the gifts will always remind them of Grandma; Mom and Dad are quiet and continue with daily activities as usual (note that it is difficult to know how they feel

because they continue with daily activities and do not express their feelings).

5. Examples: She lets the sheep loose so the family will have to look for them instead of weaving; she hides the teacher's shoe hoping the family will be called into school so they will stop weaving; each night she unravels what the family has woven.

6. Expand on the children's comments by clarifying that no matter how hard Annie wishes or how good or bad she is, she does not have the power to stop time, or her grandmother's death. Change is a natural part of life and when Annie accepts change, she is able to feel happy again. She begins weaving with happiness in her heart.

My Grandpa Died Today

Discussion Questions

1. What are some of the things Grandpa and the boy do together?

2. What might the boy be feeling when Grandpa says that he will not live forever?

3. How does the family feel after Grandpa dies and how do we know how they feel?

4. The little boy talks about a funny, empty, scary, rumbly kind of feeling at the bottom of his stomach. What do you think it is?

5. The little boy gets tired of being with sad grown-ups so he goes to his room. What does he do there to help himself feel better?

6. When the boy is playing ball, he has a rumbling feeling in his stomach but is able to make it go away. What does he do?

7. When the boy is playing ball, he figures out why his Grandfather wasn't afraid to die. Why wasn't his Grandfather afraid of death?

Possible Answers

1. Examples: They play checkers and read stories; they build models; Grandpa showed him how to hit a curve ball; Grandpa always roots for his team.

2. Examples: confused, unconcerned, disbelieving, scared.

3. The parents hold a reception and cry with the other adults. The boy's sadness and the sadness around him is so great that even the house looks like it will cry.

4. Help the children label feelings. Examples: loneliness; sadness; fear; emptiness.

5. Examples: He rolls marbles; he colors three pictures; he completes two jig-saw puzzles.

6. Explain that after people die, they are gone for always, but we have memories of them for always. Sometimes memories can make us feel happy, sometimes sad, and sometimes angry. In this situation, the boy remembers his grandfather, and memories help the boy feel happy again.

7. After the children respond, explain that Grandfather is wise and understands that all living things change and eventually die. Explain that the children should not fear change. Grandpa knows the boy has a lot more laughing and growing up to do. Grandpa knows the boy will eventually accept his grandfather's death and will take all the good things Grandpa taught him and use them.

Nana Upstairs and Nana Downstairs

Discussion Questions

1. Why does Tommy call his grandparents Nana Upstairs and Nana Downstairs?

2. What kinds of things does he do with Nana Upstairs?

3. One morning, Tommy's mother tells him some sad news. What is it?

4. How do you think Tommy feels when he finds out that Nana Upstairs has died?

5. What are some of the good memories Tommy has of Nana?

6. When Tommy is little and again when he is grown up, he sees a shooting star in the sky. What does the shooting star mean to him?

7. Does anyone have memories of someone who has died or a pet who has died?

Possible Answers

1. Because Tommy's grandmothers have the same name, he distinguishes between them by naming them Nana Upstairs and Nana Downstairs.

2. Examples: He eats candy mints with her; they sit next to each other tied up in a chair; they talk; he watches Nana Downstairs comb Nana Upstairs' hair; one time they made family movies together.

3. Tommy is told that Nana Upstairs has died.

4. After the children respond, tell them that at first Tommy is confused because he doesn't understand what "dead" means. He then becomes sad and cries when he realizes that Nana's being dead means he will not see her forever, except in memories.

5. Some fond memories are mentioned in question 2.

6. After the children respond, ask if they think it really was a kiss from Nana. Conclude by saying that no one can prove that Nana did or did not send the star, but what makes the star very special is that it is a way for Tommy to bring back fond memories of Nana.

7. Just listen and validate the children's experiences. Simply making eye contact, nodding your head, saying "uh-huh," and repeating what they have said are ways to validate feelings.

First Snow

Discussion Questions

1. What is Lien very anxious and excited to see and why?

2. What kinds of things do Lien and her grandmother do together?

3. How does Lien feel when she first hears that Grandma is dying?

4. The story doesn't discuss Lien's parents' feelings, but what do you think the parents might be feeling?

5. In the story, Lien asks both her parents what it means for Grandma to die, and neither answers her directly. How do you think she might feel?

6. What are some possible reasons why her parents do not answer Lien's question?

7. How does Lien find answers to her questions?

8. Where does Grandmother tell Lien to look for the answer and what answer does Lien find?

Possible Answers

1. She is very excited to see falling snow for the first time in her life.

2. Examples: They look at pictures of snow in a book; they sit under the covers together and talk.

3. Lien feels confused; she does not understand what dying means.

4. The parents may be feeling sad, scared, or relieved if Lien's grandmother is in a lot of pain.

5. The children may mention a range of emotions. Highlight the differences and similarities and normalize them. To normalize the responses, clarify that feelings are not right or wrong/good or bad—they just are. Examples: mad, confused, frustrated, intrigued.

6. Examples: They may be afraid and at a loss for words; it may be customary in their culture not to answer such questions and instead to allow the child to draw his or her own conclusion; they may be preoccupied when Lien asks the question.

7. Point out that Lien takes responsibility for getting her questions answered. The children, too, can take responsibility in getting their questions answered. Lien persists by asking others and herself questions until she receives an answer. The more people you ask for help, the greater the likelihood of getting help. It is important to keep trying.

8. Grandmother directs Lien to look for the answer in the snow. Lien learns that dying means to change. A snowflake falls to the ground and changes by melting into water. The drop of water then helps the plants grow, so the water has become a part of the plant. It evaporates into the air and eventually returns in the form of rain or snow. The cycle will continue.

My Grandson Lew

Discussion Questions

1. Why does Lewis awaken in the middle of the night?

2. Who comes to help Lewis?

3. What does Mother find out when she goes to Lewis's room?

4. Why is Mother surprised that Lewis remembers and misses his grandfather?

5. Mother and Lewis recall memories together. What are some of the things Mother and Lewis remember about Grandpa?

6. What do Mother and Lew discover they can do when they miss Grandpa?

7. Have any of you shared memories with another person when you felt sad? Did you feel better afterward?

Possible Answers

1. Examples: He misses his grandfather; he possibly has dreamed about his grandfather.

2. Mother.

3. Lewis misses his grandfather.

4. Lew was only two years old when his grandfather died.

5. Examples: Grandpa had a beard that scratched Lewis when they kissed each other; when Lewis would call for Grandpa in the middle of the night, Grandpa would go to Lewis's room or see what was the matter; Grandpa gave eye hugs; Grandpa's long, white robe looked like a sailboat when he walked; Grandpa would hum while holding Lewis;

Grandpa took Lewis to a museum; Lewis fell asleep in his grandfather's arms on the way home from the museum; Lewis remembers the feelings of being held in Grandpa's arms and the smell of tobacco; Grandpa laughed with happiness and said "My grandson Lewis" with pride; Grandpa said he would stay with Lewis whenever Lewis's parents went away and he did; Grandpa liked to paint.

6. Mother and Lew learn that they both think of Grandpa from time to time and that if they talk about him they won't miss him as much.

7. Just listen and validate the children's experiences. Simply making eye contact, nodding your head, saying "uh-huh," and repeating what they have said are all ways to validate feelings.

Sadako and the Thousand Paper Cranes

Discussion Questions

1. Sadako was two years old when an atom bomb was dropped on Hiroshima. Ten years later, she dies of a disease. What disease does Sadako die of?

2. How does the atom bomb give her leukemia?

3. How might Sadako feel after she is diagnosed with leukemia? Why?

4. How do you think the family feels after Sadako is diagnosed with leukemia? Why?

5. How do the family and classmates demonstrate their love and support of Sadako?

6. Leukemia is often fatal and can be painful. What does Sadako do to help herself feel better?

7. What are some of the special things about Sadako that her family and friends will remember?

8. What is the special ceremony at Peace Park held for and what is done in the ceremony?

9. What religion and rituals do Sadako's family practice?

10. How does Sadako handle the disappointment of being unable to take part in her graduation ceremony and of being unable to participate in the team race?

11. What do you think the room looks like filled with so many paper cranes?

Possible Answers

1. Sadako dies from leukemia.

2. The bomb exposes Sadako to radiation.

3. Examples: lonely, miserable, helpless. Allow the children to expand the list and do not judge their responses. Accept all answers as valid.

4. Examples: fearful, miserable, helpless. Allow the children to expand the list and do not judge their responses. Accept all answers as valid.

5. Examples: Mother comes to visit every day; Sadako's brother brings many different kinds of paper to make paper cranes; Mother brings her favorite foods to the hospital; her classmates fold 356 cranes until they reach the goal of completing 1,000 paper cranes; her classmates send her a kokeshi doll.

6. Sadako says a prayer as she folds each paper crane to help herself feel better. By setting a goal of folding 1,000 cranes, she gives herself something to work toward and can remain hopeful.

7. Examples: She loves to run and do things quickly; she loves to celebrate Peace Day; she is a happy girl; she sees good luck signs in simple daily events; she faces her illness with courage and hope.

8. Examples: The celebration is in honor of all individuals who died as a result of the atom bomb. A Buddhist Priest speaks; the people celebrating release 100 doves from cages; people set off fireworks; they carry paper lanterns to represent others who have died as a result of the atom bomb, and they launch the lanterns on the Ohta River.

9. Sadako's family is Buddhist. One of their customs is to pray, light incense, and bow their heads when at the altar.

10. Since she cannot participate with the team, she finds something that she has the ability to do.

11. This question is completely subjective. You may want to enhance the question by instructing the children to close their eyes for a moment and imagine what the hospital room looked like with so many paper cranes.

The Fall of Freddie the Leaf

Discussion Questions

1. Who are Freddie's friends and who does Freddie think is the wisest? Why?

2. What things do Freddie and his friends do together?

3. What breeze comes that appears angry to Freddie?

4. Does Freddie or any of the other leaves have any choice about dying?

5. Freddie tells Daniel that he is afraid to die. How does Daniel respond?

6. How does Daniel answer Freddie's question, "Why do we turn different colors when we are on the same tree?"

7. What does Freddie learn his purpose is?

Possible Answers

1. All the leaves are Freddie's friends; however, Freddie considers Daniel the wisest because Daniel is the biggest and has been around the longest. Daniel can answer questions that the others cannot.

2. Freddie and his friends blow in the breeze, change colors in the fall, and bask in the summer sun.

3. The winter breeze appears angry to Freddie because it is cold and strong. It also comes when the leaves have to fall and change their home. Some call it "dying."

4. No.

5. Daniel responds to Freddie's statement by explaining that "We all fear what we don't know; that is natural. . . . You were not afraid when spring turned to summer and summer turned to fall, so why should you be afraid of the season of death? . . . Life lasts forever. The tree will eventually die, but what will continue is life."

6. Daniel answers Freddie's question by explaining that "We all have had different experiences. . . . We face the sun differently and we cast shade differently."

7. Freddie's purpose is to experience life, many moons, and many suns; to be of service to the elderly and children by providing shade; to laugh and hear the laughter of others; and to change colors in the fall.

APPENDIX B

Synopses of Recommended Children's Books about Death and Dying

Three through Seven Years

Bartoli, J. *Nonna*. New York: Harvey House, 1975.

Nonna is about a young boy who learns to accept his grandmother's death. At first he refuses to believe that Nonna is gone and that she will no longer give him cookies and gifts or that she will never play with him again. Eventually new people move into Nonna's house and the boy's life goes on, but he cherishes his memories of Nonna.

Coutant, Helen. *First Snow*. New York: Alfred A. Knopf, 1974.

In *First Snow*, a young Vietnamese girl named Lien searches for the meaning of death. When she experiences her first snow, she learns that life and death are parts of the same entity by recognizing the similarities between life and snowflakes: they are both beautiful, fleeting, delicate, and changing.

DePaola, T. *Nana Upstairs and Nana Downstairs*. New York: Putnam's, 1973.

Nana Upstairs and Nana Downstairs depicts the loving relationships four-year-old Tommy has with his great-grandmother (Nana Upstairs) and his grandmother (Nana Downstairs). When Nana Upstairs dies, Tommy is very sad. His mother explains that "Nana Upstairs won't be here anymore and won't come back except in your memory." Later, when Tommy's grandmother dies, he finds comfort in his belief that both Nanas are upstairs in heaven.

Fassler, J. *My Grandpa Died Today*. Illustrated by S. Kranz. New York: Human Sciences, 1971.

In *My Grandpa Died Today*, a little boy named David tells about his beloved grandfather's death, how he feels about it, how those around him feel, and what they do. David's grandfather had taught him many things and had shared thoughts about life and death. The memories of his grandfather help David to cope with his grief and to continue his own life.

Kantrowitz, M. *When Violet Died*. New York: Parent's Magazine Press, 1973.

When Violet Died is about a family's pet bird. When the bird dies, the children plan a funeral and a memorial and invite their friends to take part in the ceremonies. Their grief is quickly resolved when they discover that Blanche, their cat, is pregnant. The author illustrates the comfort that comes from knowing that life is a continuous process.

Mellonie, Bryan, and Robert Ingpen. *Lifetimes*. New York: Bantam Books, 1983.

Lifetimes explains life and death in a simple, sensitive, and caring way. Life is referred to as the time between beginnings and endings. The book explains that all things have their own special lifetime: plants, animals, and people. The illustrations are simple and wonderful.

Zolotow, C. *My Grandson Lew*. New York: Harper and Row, 1974.

In *My Grandson Lew*, six-year-old Lew tells his mother that he misses his grandfather, who died four years previously. To her surprise, Lew's mother finds that Lew remembers many of the experiences he shared with his grandfather. Lew and his mother find comfort in sharing their memories.

Eight to Twelve Years

Bach, Marcus. *I, Monty.* **Virginia Beach: ARE Press, 1985.**

I, Monty is a unique story of a caterpillar that metamorphoses into a butterfly. The allegory explores the mysteries of life, death, rebirth, and love. The story takes place in an elementary school classroom.

Buscaglia, Leo. *The Fall of Freddie the Leaf.* **Thorofare, New Jersey: Charles B. Slack, 1982.**

The Fall of Freddie the Leaf describes how leaves change with the passing seasons, finally falling to the ground to nourish the following year's growth.

Cohen, Barbara. *Thank You, Jackie Robinson.* **New York: Lothrop, Lee and Shepard, 1974.**

Thank You, Jackie Robinson details the friendship between Sam, a fatherless boy, and Davy, a 60-year-old cook. The two are bound by their love of baseball and their interest in Jackie Robinson. After Davy's death, Sam attends the funeral, visits the cemetery, and wonders about immortality.

Dobrin, Arnold. *Scat!* **New York: Four Winds Press, 1971.**

Scat! is the story of a young boy who loves music and who is coping with the loss of his beloved grandmother. When he remembers his grandmother's words, "Listen to what your heart says . . . not your head," he plays his harmonica near her grave as a personal memorial that helps him express his sadness and helps to comfort him.

Miles, Miska. *Annie and the Old One.* **Boston: Little, Brown, 1971.**

In *Annie and the Old One*, Annie is a nine-year-old Navajo girl whose grandmother is preparing to die. Annie tries to prevent her grandmother's death, but Annie's grandmother explains that no one can prevent death. Annie learns that the whole family is part of the life cycle and that death is a part of life.

Viorst, Judith. *The Tenth Good Thing about Barney.* **New York: Atheneum, 1971.**

In *The Tenth Good Thing about Barney,* a little boy's cat named Barney dies. The boy's mother tries to comfort him by asking him to think of ten good things about Barney. He can think of only nine, but his father helps him add the tenth good thing, that Barney will now nourish the flowers.

Warburg, Sandol Stoddard. *Growing Time.* **Boston: Houghton Mifflin, 1969.**

James is lonely, angry, and sad when his old dog named King dies in *Growing Time.* Family members explain what they think happened to King after he died. James is comforted and accepts a new puppy that he had rejected earlier.

White, E. B. *Charlotte's Web.* **New York: Harper and Row, 1952.**

Charlotte's Web is a classic tale about a beautiful friendship between Wilbur the pig, Templeton the rat, and Charlotte the spider. Charlotte's death and the subsequent birth of her children help explain the cycle of life.

Twelve Years and Older

Bach, Marcus. *I, Monty.* **Virginia Beach: ARE Press, 1985.**

I, Monty is a unique story of a caterpillar that metamorphoses into a butterfly. The allegory explores the mysteries of life, death, rebirth, and love. The story takes place in an elementary school classroom.

Buscaglia, Leo. *The Fall of Freddie the Leaf.* **Thorofare, New Jersey: Charles B. Slack, 1982.**

The Fall of Freddie the Leaf describes how leaves change with the passing seasons, finally falling to the ground to nourish the following year's growth.

Coerr, Eleanor. *Sadako and the Thousand Paper Cranes.* **New York: Putnam's, 1977.**

Sadako and the Thousand Paper Cranes is a true story about a courageous Japanese girl who fights leukemia by trying to fold one thousand paper cranes. Sadako was two when the United States dropped the atom bomb on Hiroshima and dies ten years later as a result of the radiation from the bomb.

Crawford, Charles. *Three-Legged Race.* **New York: Harper & Row, 1974.**

In *Three-Legged Race,* three teenagers become friends when they are hospitalized together. Although one of them dies, the book focuses on their friendship and the concept of loss and separation. There are some references to sexuality.

Slote, Alfred. *Hang Tough, Paul Mather.* **Philadelphia: Lippincott, 1973.**

Paul, a top baseball player, becomes seriously ill in *Hang Tough, Paul Mather.* He tries to play baseball again but must return to the hospital, where a young doctor helps Paul deal with his illness and the resulting limitations. There are some references to sexuality.

APPENDIX C

Additional Books about Death

Children's Books

Death of Children

Greene, Constance. *Beat the Turtle Drum*. New York: Viking Press, 1976.

Hickman, Marcia W. *Last Week My Brother Anthony Died*. Nashville: Abingdon Press, 1984.

Johnson, Joy, and Marv Johnson. *Where's Jess?* Omaha: Centering Corporation, 1982.

Lee, Virginia. *The Magic Moth*. New York: Seabury, 1972.

Lowry, L. *A Summer to Die*. Boston: Houghton Mifflin, 1980.

Patterson, K. *Bridge to Terabithia*. New York: Crowell, 1977.

Richter, Elizabeth. *Losing Someone You Love: When a Brother or Sister Dies*. New York: Putnam's, 1986.

Rofes, Eric E. *The Kid's Book about Death and Dying*. Boston: Little, Brown, 1985.

Death of a Parent

Krementz, Jill. *How It Feels When a Parent Dies*. New York: Knopf, 1981.

Le Shan, Eda. *Learning to Say Goodbye: When a Parent Dies*. New York: Macmillan, 1978.

Facilitative and Therapeutic Books

Boulden, Jim. *Saying Goodbye*. Santa Rosa, Calif.: First Edition, 1989. Box 9358, Santa Rosa, CA 95405 (coloring book).

Heegarrd, Marge. *When Someone Very Special Dies: Children Can Learn to Cope with Grief*. Minneapolis: Woodland Press, 1988 (for people of all ages).

Books for Parents

Bach, Marcus. *I, Monty*. Virginia Beach: ARE Press, 1985.

Gaffney, Daonna, and Nal Penguin. *The Seasons of Grief: Helping Your Children Grow through Loss*. New York: New American Library, 1988.

Jampolsky, Gerald. *Good-bye to Guilt*. New York: Bantam Books, 1985.

————. *Love Is Letting Go of Fear*. Toronto: Bantam Books, 1970.

————. *Teach Only Love*. New York: Bantam Books, 1984.

Krementz, Jill. *How It Feels When a Parent Dies*. New York: Knopf, 1981.

Levine, Stephen. *Healing into Life and Death*. New York: Doubleday, 1989.

Limbot, Rana, and Sara Rich Wheeler. *When a Baby Dies: A Handbook for Healing and Helping.* La Crosse, Wis.: Resolve through Sharing, 1986.

Miller, Jack Silvey. *The Healing Power of Grief.* San Francisco: Seabury Press, 1978.

Moody, Raymond, Jr. *The Light Beyond.* New York: Bantam Books, 1989.

Morse, Melvin, and Paul Perry. *Closer to the Light: Learning from the Near Death Experiences of Children.* New York: Villard Books, 1990.

Tatelbaum, Judy. *The Courage to Grieve.* New York: Lippincott and Crowell, 1980.

Metaphysical thought and meditations
(See full references above.)

The Courage to Grieve Judy Tatelbaum

Love Is Letting Go of Fear Gerald Jampolsky

Teach Only Love Gerald Jampolsky

Good-bye to Guilt Gerald Jampolsky

I, Monty Marcus Bach

REFERENCES AND ADDITIONAL READING

Books and Articles

Aki, Mari. "Helping Children Cope with Death and Dying." Paper presented at the National Association of School Social Workers Conference, Saint Charles, Illinois, November 1989.

Brook, Barbara, Gary Silverman, and Glen Hass. "When a Teacher Dies: A School Based Intervention with Latency Children." *American Journal of Orthopsychiatry*, 55(3): 405–10.

Evans, Beth. "The Death of a Classmate: A Teacher's Experience Dealing with Tragedy in the Classroom." *Journal of School Health, Ohio* 52(2): 104–7.

Goldhaber, Dale. *Life-Span Human Development.* Orlando: Harcourt, Brace, Jovanovich: 1986.

Heegarrd, Marge. *When Someone Very Special Dies: Children Can Learn to Cope with Grief.* Minneapolis: Woodland Press, 1988. (Includes Facilitator's Guide)

Heffelfinger, Sandy. "Helping Your Students Deal with a Death." *Learning* (April 1986), 86–89.

Purkey, William, and John Novak. *Inviting School Success: A Self Concept Approach to Teaching and Learning.* Belmont, Calif.: Wadsworth, 1984.

Ross, Elisabeth Kübler. *On Death and Dying.* New York: Macmillan, 1970.

Sams, Jamie. *Sacred Path Cards: Discovery of Self through Native Teachings.* San Francisco: Harper, 1990.

Savin, Diane Lorraine. "The Expression of Mourning in an Eight Year Old Girl." *Clinical Social Work Journal.*

Staley, Betty. *Between Form and Freedom: A Practical Guide for Teenage Years.* Stroud, U.K.: Hawthorne Press, 1988.

Films

Children's Conception of Death. 30 minutes, Milwaukee School of Nursing, provided by Oakton Community College, 1978.

Death. 16-millimeter film, 40 minutes, Filmmakers Library, 1969.

ADDITIONAL RESOURCES FROM EMPOWERMENT IN ACTION....TO ENRICH YOURSELF & OTHERS

Everyday Heroes: humorous & courageous experiences shared by those living with a learning disability

By Jeanne Lagorio-Anthony LCSW (1997)

This simple and heart warming book focuses on the <u>strengths</u> developed in a person as a result of living with a learning disability. Offering hope through humor and personal stories. Providing a variety of unique perspectives, coping strategies as well as secrets to personal acceptance.
Grades 6 & up $10.00

Teen Power:
Co-authored by Karl Anthony and several other national teen speakers.(1996)
Encouragement for today's youth! Short, inspirational & motivational stories for today's teenagers.
Grades 9 & up $11.95

Pre-Teen Power:
Co-authored by Karl Anthony and several other national youth speakers. (1997)
Encouragement for today's youth! Short, inspirational & easy to read stories.
Grades 6-8 ....$11.95

MUSIC WITH A POSITIVE MESSAGE

Children of the World–Issue specific songs for elementary age children. Songs like: Don't Smoke That Cigarette, This Body is Mine & Would You Want A Kid Like You. A free Karaoke version is included for personal & party fun.
A masterpiece! ....Double Cassette $20.00, Double CD $25.00

Our World–Contemporary Rock & World beat music about global cooperation & environmental responsibility ....Cassette $10.00

Celebrate Life–Fun, esteem building sing-a-longs for kids of all ages! Includes favorites: Every Little Cell in my Body is Happy & I am Your Friend
....Cassette $10.00

TO ORDER CALL OR WRITE......**1-800-843-0165**

or

Check out our website: **www.karlanthony.com/jeanne**

Empowerment in Action
PO Box 3064, Carlsbad, CA 92009

WITHDRAWN

WITHDRAWN

Date Due

ILL 4913550 2/19/0			
AG 24 '04			
OC 25 '05			
OC 24 '07			

BRODART, CO.   Cat. No. 23-233-003   Printed in U.S.A.